ART IN NATURAL HISTORY I
Ferdinand Bauer

ART IN NATURAL HISTORY I

Ferdinand Bauer

THE AUSTRALIAN NATURAL HISTORY DRAWINGS

Marlene J. Norst

British Museum of Natural History London

First published 1989
British Museum (Natural History)
Cromwell Road
London SW7 5BD

British Library Cataloguing in Publication Data

Norst, Marlene J.
    Ferdinand Bauer: the Australian natural
    history drawings. — (Art in natural
    history; no. 1)
    1. Australian drawings. Bauer Ferdinand.
    I. Title   II. British Museum (Natural History)
    III. Series
    743.93

    ISBN 0-565-01048-4

Designed by Gillian Greenwood

Typeset by Computerised Typesetting Services Ltd, Redhill, Surrey
Printed by Craft Print Pte Ltd., Singapore

Contents

To the memory of

Ferdinand Lucas Bauer

with profound respect for his enduring genius

Acknowledgements

As a non-biologist I approached the writing of this book with some trepidation. Fortunately, the natural history experts I consulted were invariably patient and generous with their time and resources.

In particular I would like to thank Professor H. Riedl, Mrs Christa Riedl-Dorn and Dr S. Nebehay of the Natural History Museum, Vienna for making the Bauer sketches available and for much fruitful discussion; also Mrs Alice Schumacher who provided the excellent photographs. Dr Liselotte Niklas of the Botanisches Institut traced obscure bibliographic references; the Staff of the Vienna Rathaus were unfailingly courteous and efficient in providing long forgotten material and Dr Evelin Oberhammer guided me through the Liechtenstein Archives in Vienna.

The Staff of the British Museum (Natural History), all of them ardent Bauer fans, made an invaluable contribution: Nicola Round, Malcolm Beasley, Ann Datta, Judith Diment, Robert Bloomfield and above all, Rex Banks gave me encouragement, expert advice and the opportunity to realise a dream.

I am grateful to Dr W. Stearn (London) and Dr W. Lack (Berlin), who have done extensive research on Bauer, for their many helpful suggestions.

While on the research trail in London, I relied heavily on the good offices of Sylvia Fitzgerald and Lenore Thompson from the library of the Royal Botanic Gardens, Kew; and Gina Douglas of the Linnean Society of London Library. In Australia, the Staff of the Mitchell Library, Sydney, particularly Margaret Calder and Elizabeth Imashev went out of their way to assist me.

Special thanks are due to Eoin Wilkinson, Macquarie University Librarian whose invitation to lecture on Bauer first allowed me to formulate my ideas and to Jocelyn Gardner who mounted a delightful exhibition on that occasion.

For help in deciphering the Bauer letters I am indebted to friends in Vienna and Sydney. Mrs Polk, Mrs Paula Zenker and the 'English Class' of the Türkenschanz-Pensionistenheim had no difficulty in recalling the old German handwriting of their youth and Lena Cansdale in Sydney spent hours solving the difficult riddles.

Lilith Norman, Joan Nicol, Clare Dempsey and Megan Phillips deserve sincere thanks for their friendship and help; Johanna McBride, who gave me the courage to attempt the impossible and whose masterful way with the computer actually enabled us to beat the deadline, deserves a medal.

Myra Givans has been the kindest of editors. Brushing aside all difficulties, she has conquered the tyranny of distance with the ease of one of Bauer's birds.

May the book to which so many have contributed please Ferdinand Bauer's old admirers and bring him many new friends.

Kunzea baxteri

Introduction

By a curious paradox Ferdinand Lucas Bauer, widely acclaimed as one of the greatest botanical artists of all time, may well be unknown to most readers of this book. Strange, indeed, for Ferdinand Bauer undertook one of the most significant voyages ever made — with Matthew Flinders on his circumnavigation of Australia (1801–1803); his paintings and drawings of this and other journeys are treasured in museums and libraries in Liechtenstein, Oxford, Göttingen, Vienna and London, and his own contemporaries as well as botanists today compete in extolling the excellence of his work.

Various reasons can be advanced for the tragic neglect of this great artist: his failure to have most of his work published, because of the financial burden of the Napoleonic wars; the 'bilateral' amnesia occasioned by his two distinct lives, one in Austria, the other in England; his obsession with his art which allowed no space for self-promotion; and the fact that though he was both artist and scientist his work was claimed by the botanists and zoologists, stored in herbariums and natural history museums and thus became inaccessible to artists, art lovers and the public.

A few Londoners caught a brief glimpse of Ferdinand Bauer's unsurpassed water colours of Australian flowers and animals in 1959 when these formed part of an exhibition held at the British Museum (Natural History) celebrating the sesquicentenary of Darwin's birth. Then, in 1976, a magnificent volume edited by William T. Stearn and Wilfrid Blunt entitled *The Australian Flower Paintings of Ferdinand Bauer* was published by the British Museum (Natural History) and Basilisk Press. It contained 25 splendid colour reproductions of his plates but it was intended for libraries and book collectors rather than the general reader. Similarly, the British Museum (Natural History) and Alecto Historical Editions are soon to release a limited edition featuring plates prepared by Bauer for his unsuccessful publishing venture in 1813.

The present volume is a first attempt to introduce Ferdinand Bauer's work to a wider public. Since it is his Australian drawings that will allow Australians the readiest access to his art, the illustrations have been selected from the *Investigator* voyage. Most of them have never been published before. After his death the finished water colours of the Australian journey went to the Natural History section of the

Pityrodia saliaefolia, pencil sketches & finished drawing (p. 11)

British Museum while the pencil sketches were acquired by the Imperial Natural History Museum in Vienna. In the pages of this book they have, for the first time since Bauer worked on them, been reunited. It is thus possible in some instances to see how he developed a drawing from the basic sketch covered with a numeric code to indicate nuances in coloration, to the final masterpiece.

In attempting to write Bauer's biography one is confronted by a wall of silence. He was a painting, not a writing man, as the letters, which are published here for the first time, clearly show. As far as is known he kept no diaries. All those who have written about him, whether in scientific journals or biographical dictionaries, use as their main source an article published in Hooker's *London Journal of Botany* in 1843. The author was Dr Jan Lhotsky, a fellow Austrian who like Bauer had travelled to Australia bent on research. He is credited with the first serious exploration of Australia's Alps in the Kosciusko region.

Lhotsky, who was forty years younger than Ferdinand Bauer, does not appear to have met him personally but corresponded with his brother, Franz, who worked at the Royal Botanic Gardens at Kew as a natural history painter for 50 years. He also knew English naturalists for whom Ferdinand had worked and had, perhaps through Franz, obtained possession of eight letters which Ferdinand wrote in the course of the Australian voyage. These form the basis of his biographical article.

Silver box gum, *Eucalyptus pruinosa*

Lhotsky explains that what prompted him to write about Bauer was the fact that he found no mention in any of the standard reference works to 'the above named artist than whom none ever pourtrayed {sic} botanical subjects more admirably.' He, therefore, felt the need to put the record straight or as he phrased it rather more botanically and picturesquely 'to plant as it were, a cypress on the grave of a man with whom I may almost claim kindred, as my countryman and fellow-traveller in Australia.'[1]

Lhotsky first read a paper on Ferdinand Bauer at a meeting of the Linnean Society of London on 18 June 1839, 13 years after Bauer's death, and it was published in the *Proceedings* of the Society in the same year. In the covering note which Lhotsky forwarded to the Council of the Linnean Society with his article on 4 July 1839, he expresses some doubt about his ability to do justice to Bauer:

> I have bestowed much time in composing the Biography of Ferdinand Bauer, and although there can be no doubt, that if a man like f.i. [for instance] Dr. Southey (assisted moreover by Mr. Turner R.A. an eminent naturalist) would have undertaken it, it would be more valuable; yet I beg respectfully, You will not consider *who* did it, but that it is done.[2]

Four years later Lhotsky was able to provide a fuller account of Bauer's life in the seven-page article which was published in Hooker's *London Journal of Botany*.

Despite Lhotsky's brave effort, Ferdinand Bauer was so thoroughly forgotten that with rare exceptions neither he nor his work became a focus of interest for researchers. As a result, very little new biographical material has come to light. The following commentary is, therefore, based quite explicitly on Lhotsky's biographical sketch of 1843 which is presented here in italics. It approximates most closely to oral history and so will provide, one hopes, a more authentic note since Lhotsky, though he did not know Bauer personally, at least knew those who did. My comments are merely intended to explain or to add information which has become available in the intervening 145 years — most of it in the last decade. Particularly significant is the detailed work which has recently been devoted to the journals of participants in the *Investigator* voyage, such as Captain Matthew Flinders, Robert Brown, the botanist and Peter Good, the gardener. Their journals have helped me to reconstruct the Australian diary which Bauer never wrote and to relate, from his perspective, the main events of the Australian odyssey. Lhotsky omitted these in his account because he knew that in 1843 his readers, predominantly English botanists, were still fully conversant with all the details of Flinders' voyage.

It may be incomprehensible that Ferdinand Bauer should, in 1988, need to be redeemed from oblivion but since that is the case it would seem reasonable to let the work itself plead his cause. Since Bauer's pictures constitute his claim to be honoured as a cultural hero, this book has deliberately chosen to focus attention on them rather than on his poorly documented biography. Ferdinand Bauer belonged to that rare species for whom living and creating powerful visual images is a single, seamless process. We have no written records of his reflections on that process. They may be lost or it may simply not have been in his nature to seek an alternative form of self-expression. It is also part of the whole Bauer paradox that though he belonged to a family of painters, there is no known portrait of him.

Perhaps it is fortunate that circumstances have conspired to shroud the artist but reveal his art. We may, in the end, find that a study of Bauer's pictures — in itself immensely rewarding — will also lead us by the most direct path to an understanding of the man.

Feldsberg (Liechtenstein Archives, Vienna)

Artistic Apprenticeship

Ferdinand Bauer was born in 1760, at Feldsperg in Austria, where his father held the appointment of Painter to the court of the reigning Prince of Lichtenstein, but died, when his son Ferdinand was only a year old.[1]

Feldsberg, in the northern part of Lower Austria, was one of the most important possessions of the Princes of Liechtenstein whose castle, built on the foundations of an old border fortress, dominated the town. When Jan Lhotsky was preparing his biographical sketch of Ferdinand Bauer, he sent a preliminary draft to Ferdinand's brother, Franz, at Kew for checking. The only correction the latter found it necessary to make was, in fact, to the birth place:

> I find the facts all very correct only the name of our birth place Feldsperg which is stated to be in Moravia but should be Austria and I have taken the liberty to mark it so in Your Ms.[2]

As if to prove Lhotsky right in retrospect, the peace treaty of 1919 which followed on World War I and the disintegration of the Austro-Hungarian Empire, incorporated Feldsberg in the new state of Czechoslovakia. It was renamed Valtice.

Ferdinand's father, Lucas Bauer, took up his position as Court Painter about 1744 and is known to have received commissions for several religious paintings. Ferdinand was the youngest child in the family and together with two older brothers Josef Anton (1756-?) and Franz Andreas (1758-1840) had inherited their father's artistic talent. Josef, who had been sent by the Prince of Liechtenstein to further his art studies in Rome, returned to take up the position his father had previously held as court painter and inspector of the Liechtenstein Galleries in Vienna.

> *In his earliest youth, Ferdinand copied plants and birds from the designs of his late parent, but soon he took to painting from nature, and followed her as his chief guide throughout life. In the year 1775 we find him connected with the Rev. N. Boccius, Superior of the convent and hospital* Fratrum Misericordiae *at Feldsperg; who, being very fond of botanical studies, employed F. Bauer to make miniature delineations of plants from nature. He executed the greater part of a collection, which, consisting of 16 volumes in folio, may yet be seen in the Prince's library at Vienna. Occasionally Ferdinand resided in that city, painting landscapes in the studio of the celebrated Artist, Professor Brand.[3]*

Blackwattle, *Callicoma serratifolia*   *Lomandra hastilis*

Some sources[4] refer to Ferdinand's mother, Theresia, as having guided his first artistic attempts but Lhotsky is certainly right in attributing Bauer's development as a botanical artist to Boccius. Norbert Boccius (1729-1806) was not only the prior of the monastery, he was also a qualified medical man with strong botanical interests which led him to lay out a fine botanical garden within the monastery walls and to embark on records in miniature. All three of Lucas' artistic sons, Josef, Franz and Ferdinand contributed to this series of 2750 miniatures and the title of the work acknowledges their contribution: *Norbert Bossio collectas et a Josepho, Francisco et Ferdinando Bauer pictas.* Ferdinand was only 15 when his first drawing was published. The collection was eventually acquired by the Princedom and is today to be found in the Liechtenstein Gallery in Vaduz, Liechtenstein. Dr Walter Lack is presently preparing these miniatures for publication.

In about 1780 Franz and Ferdinand Bauer moved to Vienna where they began to work for Baron Nicolaus von Jacquin (1727-1817), Professor of Botany and Chemistry at Vienna University and Director of the University's botanic garden. Dutch by birth, Jacquin spent his life in Vienna and was acknowledged as one of the greatest botanists of the age as well as an accomplished artist. He carried on a wide correspondence with scientists from all over Europe and was on particularly friendly terms with Sir Joseph Banks whom he describes in one of his letters as a 'second father' to his son, Joseph, during the latter's stay in London. Jacquin set the Bauer brothers to work on the illustrations for his book of rare plants *Icones Plantarum Rariorum*, which appeared in three volumes from 1751 to 1793. This period of apprenticeship proved invaluable. Jacquin fostered their extraordinary talent for observation by introducing them to microscopic work and they mastered the art of accurately portraying even the minutest detail. Later in London, Franz was to be particularly esteemed for his knowledge and skill in microscopic work demonstrated in publications like his *Microscopical observations on Red Snow*.

> *It was in 1784 that Dr. John Sibthorp of Oxford arrived in Vienna, with the view of examining the unique manuscripts of Dioscorides in the Imperial Library. Having been introduced by Nicholas Jacquin to Pater Boccius, Dr. Sibthorp first met Bauer at Feldsperg, and the former was so much pleased with the young artist's performances that he engaged him as a Natural History painter, to accompany him on a voyage which he then was about to undertake in Greece. They accordingly started the same year, proceeding through Italy to Constantinople where they spent the winter, and devoted the time to 1787, to visiting Athens, Corinth, the Greek Islands and Cyprus; Bauer delineating both plants. and landscapes . . . but Bauer possessed too discerning and unprejudiced a mind, not to perceive that he could never attain any eminence by merely copying plants even with the most mechanical accuracy; and it was, most probably, during his travels with Dr. Sibthorp, that he had devoted himself to the true study of Botany as a science, since several of the plants, for instance* Veronica glauca, Ziziphora capitata *and* Salvia crassifolia, *are mentioned as discoveries of his; and especially in the Isle of Cyprus he appears to have been eminently diligent and successful.* [5]

John Sibthorp, like his father before him, was Sherardian Professor of Botany at Oxford University and only two years older than Ferdinand Bauer. He was eager to revive the herbal lore of ancient Greece and his visit to Vienna was prompted by the need to engage in the necessary preliminary research. The Imperial library possessed the *Codex Vindobonensis*, one of the few manuscripts in existence which allowed a first-hand study of the work of Dioscorides. It was quite natural that in the course of his studies in Vienna Sibthorp should have visited Nicolaus von Jacquin with whom he had, undoubtedly, been in correspondence and that he should have asked him for advice about a botanical artist to accompany him on his field work in the Mediterranean. Perhaps Jacquin would not have been quite so helpful had he known that his suggestion was going to cost him the services of Ferdinand and Franz, both of whom were subsequently to be taken over by Sir Joseph Banks in London.

Sibthorp's party seems to have left in the spring of 1786 and included John Hawkins, Sibthorp's brother-in-law with whom Ferdinand formed a lasting friendship. The relationship with Sibthorp himself, however, seems to have been rather more problematic. They returned to England in December 1787, Ferdinand having, in 18 months, produced over 1500 sketches.

Hibbertia dealbata

On their return to England, it was highly gratifying to Bauer to find his brother Francis settled as botanical painter to His Britannic Majesty, King George III., at Kew; and he now devoted the chief part of his time to finishing the drawings made for Dr. Sibthorp's Flora Graeca, . . . *Dr. Sibthorp having died, Sir James Edward Smith published, in the year 1806, the first volume of the* Flora Graeca, *mentioning in his preface the merits of our friend in a most honourable manner: Pictorem egregii nominis, Ferdinandum Bauer, cujus virtutem icones nostrae exhibent, secum duxit* (Sibthorp took with him a painter of excellent reputation, Ferdinand Bauer, whose merits our illustrations demonstrate) . . . *We think we may venture to point to the* Salvia pomifera, Morina Persica, *and* Saccharum Ravennae, *as patterns of botanical iconography, which, though executed long ago, in an early part of the work, remain unsurpassed to the present day.*[6]

Pleiogynium solandri

In 1788 Franz Bauer set out with Jacquin's son, Joseph, on a European grand tour which was intended to take them to England and eventually to France. Jacquin did continue on to Paris which he reached in the turmoil of the revolution but Franz was persuaded by Sir Joseph Banks to accept a position as botanical artist in Kew Gardens at a salary of £300 per annum. He took up the position in 1790 (not 1788, as Lhotsky suggests), in time became a member of the Royal Society and remained at Kew until his death 50 years later. Sir Joseph obviously thought very highly of Franz Bauer and remembered him in his will:

> On condition that he continues to reside on Kew Green, and employs himself in making drawings of plants that flower in the collection at Kew, in the same manner as he has hitherto done.[7]

Among the Vienna autographs held by the Science Library of University College, London I recently discovered the unsigned draft of a letter from Jacquin senior to Sir Joseph Banks which is dated 17 April 1790. After expressing his gratitude to Sir Joseph for the latter's kindness to his son, Jacquin mentions the Bauers and hopes that Franz 'may continue giving you satisfaction by his works.' Though only half way through his own work, he appears not to have begrudged Sir Joseph the services of his best illustrators, but perhaps there is just a slight edge to the comment which immediately follows:

> *Instead of the Brothers Bauer I have at present here a young man who from a cook to a convent of monks is become a painter by his sole genius and without being taught by a Master, who begins already to follow the traces of the Bauers as you will find by my Icones.*[8]

The reference here is to Johannes Scharf who worked for Jacquin from 1790 till his death in 1794.[9]

In a letter dated 21 May 1792, in Kew Library, Franz Bauer writing in German to Jacquin's son, Joseph, refers to Ferdinand, remarking that Dr Sibthorp and Mr Hawkins had planned another trip to Greece but that, at the last moment, Sibthorp had pulled out because he was busy with several large properties he had recently acquired 'as a result Ferdinand will not be going either but will continue with his work this summer.' Sibthorp did return to Greece once more in 1794 but then, too, Ferdinand remained in Oxford, completing the illustrations—some 1000 water colours of plants, 363 of animals and 131 of landscapes. The first volume of the *Flora Graeca* appeared in 1806 but the last of the ten volumes was not published till 1840 after both Sibthorp and Bauer had died. It contained a text by James Edward Smith and John Lindley and 966 plates by Ferdinand which had been engraved by the renowned James Sowerby. Sibthorp had left sufficient money in his will for the publication of this magnificent work which was sold at a considerable loss. The original drawings are now in Oxford and Göttingen and include many, especially landscape and animal studies, which have never been published. Joseph Dalton Hooker, the eminent British botanist, called the *Flora Graeca* 'the greatest botanical work that has ever appeared.'[10]

Australian Adventure

But even before the Flora Graeca *was published, so early as year 1801, we find the merits of our friend fully acknowledged, and himself appointed Natural History Draughtsman to the expedition to Terra Australis, commanded by Captain Flinders, of "H.M.S. Investigator" . . . His salary was £300 a year, with rations for himself and servant. The E.I. (East India) Company having contributed £1200 towards the expenses of this expedition, the share which Bauer received, enabled him to make his outfit as an artist, very complete. It was further granted, by the Lords of the Admiralty, that all the drawings executed, which were not required for publication in any work connected with the expedition, should be the artist's own property, as well as the specimens collected by him, except those that should go to the British Museum.*[1]

The work on the *Flora Graeca* and his brother's activities at Kew had certainly made Ferdinand Bauer well known in England. The scientists were a closely-knit community and a good illustrator was highly prized. When Sir Joseph Banks decided to mount an expedition under the command of Captain Matthew Flinders to complete the detailed surveying of the Australian coastline and study the flora and fauna, he seems to have chosen Ferdinand as one of his 'gentlemen of science' without a moment's hesitation. This, in spite of the fact that Ferdinand was a foreigner and almost twice as old as any one else on board including the Captain.

On 19 January 1801 Matthew Flinders was commissioned as Lieutenant-in-command (later Commander) of H.M. Sloop *Investigator*. The ship had originally been a collier, the *Fram*, and had been bought by the Navy in 1798, refitted as a sixteen gun war-ship and re-christened H.M.S. *Xenophon*. Renamed once again on 19 January, she was this time refitted according to Sir Joseph Banks' specifications to prepare her for her great voyage of investigation. Sir Joseph had sailed with Cook on the *Endeavour* (1768-1771) when the east coast of New Holland was first explored. He was extremely knowledgable about Australia and a most influential figure in scientific and naval circles.

Ferdinand Bauer was appointed to work under the direction of Robert Brown, a medical practitioner and botanist. His appointment dated from 10 February, 1801 and his salary was eventually increased to 300 guineas. A servant called Powel was assigned to him who, sadly, remains invisible in all accounts of the voyage though he seems to have remained with Bauer until 1805.

On 29 April the participants in this adventure signed a contract with the Admiralty. They were Robert Brown, naturalist, Ferdinand Bauer, botanic drafts-man, William Westall, landscape and figure draftsman, Peter Good, gardener and John Allen, miner. The astronomer John Crosley signed the contract later, but because of illness had to return home when the expedition reached the Cape of Good Hope. The gentlemen were considered as supernumeraries to a crew of 88 whom *The Times* of 27 June 1801 described as being 'distinguished by a glazed hat decorated with a globe and the name of the ship in letters of gold.'

The *Investigator* spent three months in the English port of Sheerness, being adapted for her new role. Unfortunately, the placement of the gunports in her previous existence had considerably weakened her timbers and she was to suffer from chronic leaks and consequent dampness and mould throughout the voyage. On 2 June, after suffering a slight mishap by running on to a sandbank near Folkestone, she finally docked at Spithead. Here, on the morning of 15 June, Brown, Bauer and Westall, who had travelled together in the coach from London to Portsmouth on the previous afternoon, finally boarded her. They found their servants already waiting for them.

While the accommodation on ship was fairly cramped, the scientists were particularly well equipped for their mission. Not only did they have a collection of Australian specimens, a greenhouse and an Ellis aquatic microscope, but they also had a large library of books dealing with South Sea voyages which was housed in the former gunroom. Sir Joseph Banks had even lent them his copy of *The Endeavour Journal* which he had written on Cook's voyage. They carried provisions for 18 months which included a plentiful supply of lime-juice and sauerkraut against the dreaded scurvy as well as a quantity of livestock — pigs, goats, fowls, hunting dogs and two cats, Van and the redoubtable Trim, the Captain's cat to whom a statue was recently raised near the Mitchell Library in Sydney.

The expedition did not set sail until 18 July 1801 and in the intervening month Brown and Bauer made excursions to nearby places like Southsea where they collected seaweed and to the Isle of Wight. Here they had the company of Ann Flinders who had married the Captain three months before. She was herself 'a competent botanical artist . . . (and) found in Bauer much to admire both as an artist and a friend to herself and Matthew.'[2] In a letter to Ann sent from Spithead on 7 July Flinders writes: 'The gentle Mr. Bauer seldom forgets to add "and Mrs. Flinders' good health" after the cloth is withdrawn.'[3]

The Voyage to Australia: 18.7.1801 — 6.12.1801

Having finally set sail the *Investigator* headed for the Madeiras which were sighted on 31 July. Brown in his autograph diary reports that Flinders caught a turtle which Bauer drew. Next day they anchored and a small party including Brown and Bauer set off in the cutter to explore Bujio in the Dezertas Islands which they found to be as

Leschenaultia formosa

barren as the name implies. In Funchal, the Portuguese Governor gave them permission to live on shore but they found the accommodation in the hotel far worse than on the ship. Flinders notes in his journal that 'our gentlemen complained of it being miserable enough and the swarms of fleas etc. by night were not an agreable addition.'[4] Peter Good in his journal gives a vivid account of an excursion lasting four days during which they made an unsuccessful attempt to climb to the summit of the 6056 ft volcanic Pico Riuvo. Botanically, however, the excursion was a great success. They added to their collection and were much impressed by the cultivation of grapes, peaches and figs in the area. During the time in the Madeiras the *Investigator* underwent the first of many re-caulking sessions.

After leaving on 7 August and passing the Cape Verde Islands they crossed the equator. The celebrations that accompanied this event were, according to Good, 'Drunk and turbulent'. They then sailed north of Trinidad where they saw whales and many birds, including the albatross, cape pigeons and cape hens, before reaching the Cape of Good Hope on 16 October. They anchored in Simon's Bay to the accompaniment of whales throwing themselves 'entirely out of the water and such an enormous bulk falling into the water made a noise like the report from a musket.'[5] They found six other ships already in port and so were able to despatch their first letters. They remained there for 18 days to take on supplies and get further repairs done to the vessel which was already beginning to leak badly.

This lengthy stay gave the scientists ample opportunity for their field work. But the time still seemed too short. Peter Good reports for 17 October:

> went ashore in morning in Company with Mr. Brown Bawer and Allen and Collected a great variety of fine plants Some insects and minerals — The plants for variety and beauty were beyond description some I had never seen before particularly Orchis Drosera and Hemimeris and many I had never seen in flower returned on Board at about 6 P.M. loaded[6]

Although he is not mentioned by name, one would hope that Bauer was also witness to a remarkable intercultural event which occurred on 18 October when Good reports that they were led by Mr Ryley, surgeon of the *Lancaster*, 'to a house where we found an assembly of Hottentots dancing Scotch reels to Scotch Tunes on the Violin.'[7]

On 24 October the scientists set out early for Capetown and, on losing their way, were offered hospitality in a grand house called 'Tokay' owned by Johann Loos, a German. Next day they attempted to climb Table Mountain but were forced back from the summit by fog and rain and spent the night in Capetown. In the morning Brown and Good made a second unsuccessful attempt, while Bauer, Westall and Bell, the ship's surgeon decided to make straight for the cutter. On the return journey, Bell and Westall lost their bearings but had the good fortune to end up at Tokay again; while Bauer found his way back to the cutter alone but arriving too late to go on board spent the night sharing a tent with the ailing John Crosley. Reading Peter Good's account one is left with the impression that this excursion in the fog turned into a complicated game of blind man's buff.

None of these adventures are mentioned by Bauer in the two letters to his brother Franz sent from the Cape of Good Hope. He is however delighted by the flowers, especially by the orchids which he knows are his brother's special love — 'I wish I could send you to England all the orchid types which I have seen so far.'[8] In his second letter he remarks that the excursion over Table Mountain was arduous but he was pleased that he had undertaken it because of the beauty of the plants — 'above all the Orchitis Proteax'. He adds 'today the 3rd of November, it has been decided to depart for King George Sound, New Holland. I must admit, however, that I am not happy to be leaving this area so soon because of the great number of beautiful things which could be found here, if one had more time to look for them.'[9]

Australian sea lions, *Neophoca cinerea*

Cape Leeuwin to Sydney: 5.1.1802 — 9.5.1802

In heavy seas with gale force winds blowing they set off next morning. Five weeks later, on 6 December at 7 pm, they had their first sight of New Holland, when they approached the south-west coast of what is today Western Australia. Flinders named Cape Leeuwin in honour of the Dutch ship which had first called there in 1622. Two days later they anchored in King George Sound and explored Seal Island where they camped overnight. The *Investigator* then moved to the excellent Princess Royal Harbour which is today the Port of Albany. Here they spent an eventful month, but Bauer again gives only a very sparse account. 'Remained there till 4

January, 1802 during which time we made a number of short land excursions in the course of which we found many new plants.'[10]

In fact, they collected 500 species of plants in King George Sound and saw, to name but a few, Cape Barren geese, wild ducks, parakeets, snakes, seals and their first emus and kangaroo. One of their most exciting excursions was organised by Flinders for 23/24 December. From the top of Mount Clarence he had sighted two lagoons near West Cape Howe and sent a party to search for fresh water. Gentlemen, servants and hunting dogs had a most exhausting time of it in the burning sun. They trudged for two days through thick brushwood, waded knee deep in morasses and scrambled over rugged hills. The lagoon they found on the first day provided them with refreshing pure water but the water in the second lagoon proved to be brackish. When they eventually climbed to the top of the hills, they were totally parched. Peter Good takes up the story:

> We had not returned far when Mr. Bawer was so much overcome with fatigue and want of water that he could not proceed — Mr. Brown as also a Sailor and I continued with him while the others proceeded for the Ship where they arrived about 9 very much exhausted — Mr. Bawer having rested awhile we again proceeded intending at any rate to search some water if possible of which we were so much in want — but he was frequently obliged to sit down — we could find no water till about midnight we arrived on the Beach and soon came to known spring which was drank with delight — we then proceeded to the Tents where we slept sound till morning.[11]

The water and the tents must have seemed to Ferdinand, used to celebrating Christmas on the 24th of December, as the best Christmas gifts of all. The New Year began well for him when on 1 January 1802, he found the pitcher plant (*Cephalotus follicularis*).

They sailed from Albany on 5 January and three days later reached the Archipelago of Recherche which Flinders treated with great respect — 'a collection of more dangers than this archipelago presents in a single space is seldom found.'[12] The scientists, however, were delighted with Lucky Bay and Flinders granted their request to stay for four days to allow them to collect their specimens. They gathered a good harvest. Only the cycad palm proved their undoing. They split open the luscious looking fruit and ate the seeds which acted as an emetic. Peter Good reports the consequences in detail and also proves that the library had not been used to full advantage. 'Captain Cook relates a similar instance which occurred to his crew and on giving the fruit to the Hogs they swelled and died.'[13]

Another remarkable event Peter Good relates concerns a shark they caught a few days later. On opening it up they found that it had eaten two whole seals and swallowed a native spear as well. They spent two days on Goose Island named for the Cape Barren geese which were found there and Flinders climbed to the summit of the peak which was later called after him. Bauer in his letter of 22 May from Sydney comments on the widespread bushfires which they noticed in the area.

On 28 January they entered the waters of the Great Australian Bight, so named later by Flinders using the word 'Australia' as part of a place name for the first time.

Pitcher plant, *Cephalotus follicularis*

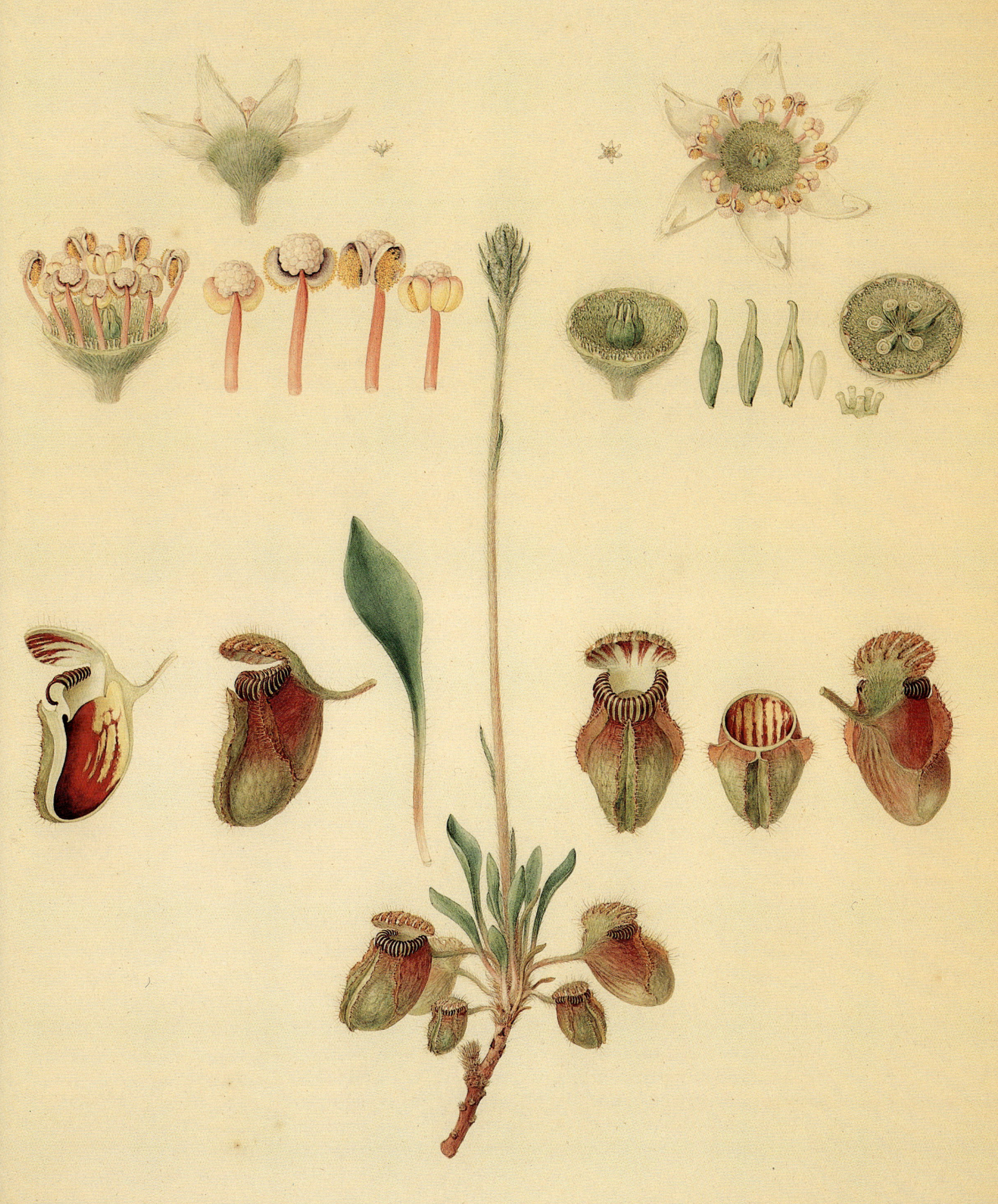

Common ringtailed possum, *Pseudocherius peregrinus*

At Petrel Bay they had their first encounter with the mutton birds or sooty petrels. In the intense heat, it was 98°F in the shade, Flinders reports that they frequently sank into the deep holes made by the birds and fell onto the sand. The country was parched. Later, on the Isle of St Peter (now Goat Island) they found many Tamor wallabies.

Flinders made a running survey of the treacherous coastline. Leaving the coast during the night and returning in the morning he threaded his way between the many small islands and rocky outcrops.

> . . . on the 5th of Feb. 1802, an honour was conferred upon him (Bauer) that promised to perpetuate his memory. 'To the south-east of Franklin's island, at the distance of eleven miles, there is a low projection of the main land to which the name of Point Brown was given, in compliment to the naturalist; and four leagues farther, in the same line, a cliffy head received the appellation of Cape Bauer, after the painter of Natural History.'[14] Such names are frequently changed by subsequent navigators, and it is with the view to obviate this possibility, that Governor Franklin, during his stay at Tasman's peninsula, issued orders that, in all official surveys, the original appellations, as bestowed by the earliest authentic discoverers, should always be preserved.[15]

Unfortunately in Ferdinand Bauer's case, Franklin's precautions were not entirely successful. The patriotic fervour of World War I caused this German sounding name to be replaced by the name Wondoma and though by a 1925 edict the old name was officially restored, many maps today have not restored Bauer's Cape to him. Even the 1984 edition of *The Times Atlas* shows the name as Wondoma.

Bauer in his letter from Sydney makes no mention of the honour conferred on him nor does he mention an odd incident which occurred on 21 February when Flinders caught a carpet snake and 'Thistle with sail needle and twine sowed up his mouth.'[16]

The *Investigator* next anchored at Uncertain Island later to be renamed Thistle's Island for the Master who together with seven others lost his life when setting out to find water and to make soundings in one of the *Investigator's* two cutters. The boat disappeared in a reef of breakers when three miles out from the ship and the crew were presumably taken by sharks. Ferdinand reports on this tragic accident. 'We would have considered ourselves fortunate . . . if we had not had the misfortune to lose the master of our ship, Mr. Thistle, a midshipman Mr. Taylor and six sailors.'[17] He makes no mention of the Aborigines they met and merely says 'we found very few inhabitants on this land and none at all on the islands, if we do not want to count the kangaroos among them of which we found very many on the islands.'[18]

At Memory Cove near Port Lincoln, which like Cape Catastrophe was named in honour of the lost crew members, Bauer drew the blue, green and yellow banded parrot which was later to be named after him, *Psitticus baueri*. Known today as the Port Lincoln ringneck, *Barnardius zonarius*, Bauer's illustration can be seen on page 119.

They spent ten days in Port Lincoln, the only sheltered natural harbour to be found in that region and met Aborigines who looked as though they might want to make contact given more time. Flinders makes an interesting comment on the occasion: 'Such seemed to have been the conduct of these Australians: . . . I am persuaded that their appearance on the morning the tents were struck was a prelude to their coming down; and that had we waited a few days longer, a friendly communication would have ensued.'[19]

On 8 March they entered Spencer's Gulf and two days later were climbing in the mountain range later to be called by Edward John Eyre, the Flinders' Ranges. Brown, Bauer, Westall, their servants and Good landed on the eastern shore, walked 15 miles and at 5 pm that afternoon reached the summit of the highest peak, later to be known as Mount Brown, where they spent the night. It was a very arduous journey where, once again, they suffered from lack of water but their reward was a splendid view across the coastal plain. It had by now become quite clear that there was no passage running from the south coast to the Gulf of Carpentaria in the north as had been thought possible. Australia was one single continent.

On 20 March they sighted Kangaroo Island, situated at the mouth of St Vincent Gulf. The cutter was lowered and Flinders, the botanists and the ever faithful hunting dogs were landed. They found so many specimens that Brown asked for permission to return the next day. This was a fateful expedition for the kangaroo. The indigenous kangaroo called after Flinders, *Macropus flindersi fuliginosus*, was slaughtered for meat and for study, Flinders gives the following account:

> After this butchery, for the poor animals suffered themselves to be shot in the eyes, and in some cases to be knocked on the head with sticks, the whole ship's company was employed this afternoon, in skinning and cleaning the kanguroos; and a delightful regale they provided, after four months privation from almost any fresh provisions.[20]

Kangaroo, *Macropus* sp., head

Kangaroo, *Macropus* sp., foetus

Rock-wallaby, *Petrogale* sp., details

They also shot a 'wumat (wombat) . . . those little bear-like quatrupeds.'[21] Bauer has sketches of kangaroos from this period and also a very moving sketch of a kangaroo foetus.

They stayed on Kangaroo Island for three days, then crossed the Investigator Strait and entered St Vincent's Gulf, returning to anchor at Kangaroo Island where they killed a number of seals. Flinders comments: 'The seal . . . seemed to be much the more discerning animal of the two; for its actions bespoke of knowledge of our not being kanguroos, whereas the kanguroos not infrequently appeared to consider us to be seals.'[22]

Four days were spent in Nepean Bay where, in the lagoon later named Pelican Lagoon, Flinders describes an encounter with these birds:

> Flocks of old birds were sitting upon the beaches of the lagoon, and it appeared that the islands were their breeding places; not only so, . . . it should seem that they had for ages been selected for the closing scene of their existence . . . nor can anything be more consonant to the feelings, if pelicans have any, than quietly to resign their breath, whilst surrounded by their progeny, and in the same spot where they first drew it. Alas, for the pelicans! Their golden age is passed; but it has much exceeded in duration that of man.[23]

On 8 April the historic meeting with the French ship *Le Géographe* took place in what was later to be named Encounter Bay to commemorate the occasion. Bauer was quite aware of the political and scientific rivalry between England and France when he reported: 'We met . . . [the Géographe] with Capt. Baudin which was travelling on an English passport for the same purpose as the Investigator.'[24]

The *Investigator* had now reached that part of the coast which today belongs to the State of Victoria. On 22 April they crossed Bass Strait separating mainland Australia from Tasmania and two days later Bauer together with the other scientists landed on King Island where they found fresh water and eight new species of ferns including tree ferns. Brown and Good were so engrossed in their collecting that they very nearly missed the boat which had to fire two guns to alert them to the fact that she was leaving.

They reached Port Phillip on 26 April which, unknown to them, had been discovered ten weeks earlier by Captain John Murray. They stayed for five days on the Mornington Peninsula and two parties set out to explore the area. Bauer, Good and Allen went south while Flinders, Brown and Westall investigated the area east of the bay and climbed the bluff known as Arthur's Seat. It was gently undulating country which reminded Good of 'a Gentlemans Park in England being covered with fine Green grass and Numerous Trees and Bushes in pleasing irregularity.'[25] Here, Bauer found a richly decorated Aboriginal club known as a waddy, but few plants that they had not seen before. He also made a sketch of the Rainbow lorikeet, *Trichoglossus haematodus*, which he found in this area.

On 1 May the *Investigator* headed for Wilson's Promontory and passed the Kent Group of islands. The wombat they captured there is possibly the one which was to survive and be finally taken back alive to England on the *Investigator* in 1805. Flinders was now in waters that were very familiar to him from his travels with Bass on his previous visit to Australia. The *Investigator* sailed past Cape Howe reaching Port Jackson on Sunday 9 May and at 3 pm anchored in Sydney Cove after a journey that had lasted 295 days. Two days later she was moored at Benelong Point which is today the site of the Sydney Opera House.

While the boat was being repaired during their six weeks' stay in Sydney, the scientists lived on shore and made a number of excursions to the Grose, Nepean and Hawkesbury rivers. Two Aborigines, Bungaree who had been on a voyage with Flinders during his previous visit to Australia and Nanbaree joined the crew and a new master, John Aken was chosen to replace John Thistle.

Bauer seems to have waited for 12 days before despatching a letter to his brother

Wombats, *Vombatus ursinus*

Franz on 22 May, but then sent another one off on 20 July, the night before they were due to sail out of Sydney Harbour 'bound for the east coast and the Gulf of Carpentaria in the north.'[26]

In this letter he mentions four excursions: one to Richmond on 3 June; one to the Hawkesbury stopping the night at Parramatta on 17 June; and one to North Rock on 18 June. Then, on 22 June, they sailed up the Grose River to the Falls, left the boat and, helped by a guide, went to the foot of the Blue Mountains. They climbed part of the first range before returning by way of the Hawkesbury River on board the *Lady Nelson*, a companion ship which had been selected for inshore work. Bauer reports that his sketches now number 700 and that he has left them with Governor King for safe keeping.

Kookaburra, *Dacelo leachii*

During this time two letters were sent to Sir Joseph Banks in London, one by Flinders, the other by Brown, both singing Bauer's praises. Flinders writing on 20 May says: 'It is fortunate for science that two men of such assiduity and abilities as Mr. Brown and Mr. Bauer have been selected: their application is beyond what I have been accustomed to see.'[27] Brown writing on 30 May reports that Bauer has made 350 plant sketches and 100 of animals 'he has indeed been indefatigable and has bestowd infinite pains on the dissections of the parts of fructification of the plants.'[28] Brown also wrote to Dr Dryander, Banks' librarian, and to the Right Honourable C. F. Greville informing them that 750 botanical specimens had been collected on the south coast, of which about 300 were new. These were stored in the ship's bread room where they were unfortunately susceptible to mould and rats. On 21 July the *Investigator* left Port Jackson together with her companion ship, the *Lady Nelson* and sailed up the east coast.

Sydney to the Gulf of Carpentaria: 21.7.1802 — 3.11.1802

After reaching the present Queensland coast they came to Fraser Island, one of the largest sand islands in the world, which is covered with rain forest. Here the

Kookaburra, *Dacelo leachii*

scientists had some time for botanising. On 6 August they discovered Port Curtis and made excursions to Facing Island, Cape Capricorn and Cape Keppel.

Near Cape Keppel a group of Aborigines rescued two of the *Investigator* crew who had lost their way.

> [They had taken] our two forlorn people . . . & offered them roasted Ducks & fish
> & afterwards led them to the Beach which they were very near although they did
> not think so till they saw it & believed they would not have reached it for several
> hours but for the friendly assistance of the Natives, Mr. Evans being very Thirsty
> made Signal as if to drink the Salt water when they made a dolefull noise very
> expressive of sorrow & immediately led him to fresh water . . . They were the
> strongest made Natives we had Seen in New Holland painted with a great variety
> of figures & colours wore necklaces of reed & shells & had a great variety of
> features some were thought upwards of 6 feet high.[29]

The *Investigator* stopped at Harvey's Isles, Port Bowen which was covered with indigenous hoop pine and at Shoalwater Bay which had been named by Cook. They reached this bay on 25 August in very hot and humid weather thinking it was an island. In spite of the heat the scientists proceeded to climb the highest peak and were rewarded by a splendid view of Shoalwater Bay and the eastern islands covered with Norfolk pines. They also realized that they were not on an island after all. Here Bauer sketched a bandicoot and drew several sketches of a kookaburra.

Eucalyptus lehamanni

On 14 September Bauer, Westall and Good with a large party set off for a three-day excursion to the hills which were five miles distant. They found the country to be barren, flat and lightly timbered. They saw kangaroos, found fresh water and 'returned with a tolerable harvest.'[30]

While Flinders was busy surveying from the deck of the *Lady Nelson*, the scientists together with Bungaree spent the beginning of September botanising and making friendly contact with the local Aborigines. The area was well covered with eucalypts and pine trees. On Flinders' return, the *Investigator* entered Thirsty Sound on 5 September and here they saw water snakes which Bauer promptly sketched. They then moved on into Broad Sound where Bauer was stung by a tree, *Tragiodes pruriens*, a beautiful tree with red berries. Ever the artist, his pain did not prevent him from sketching it.

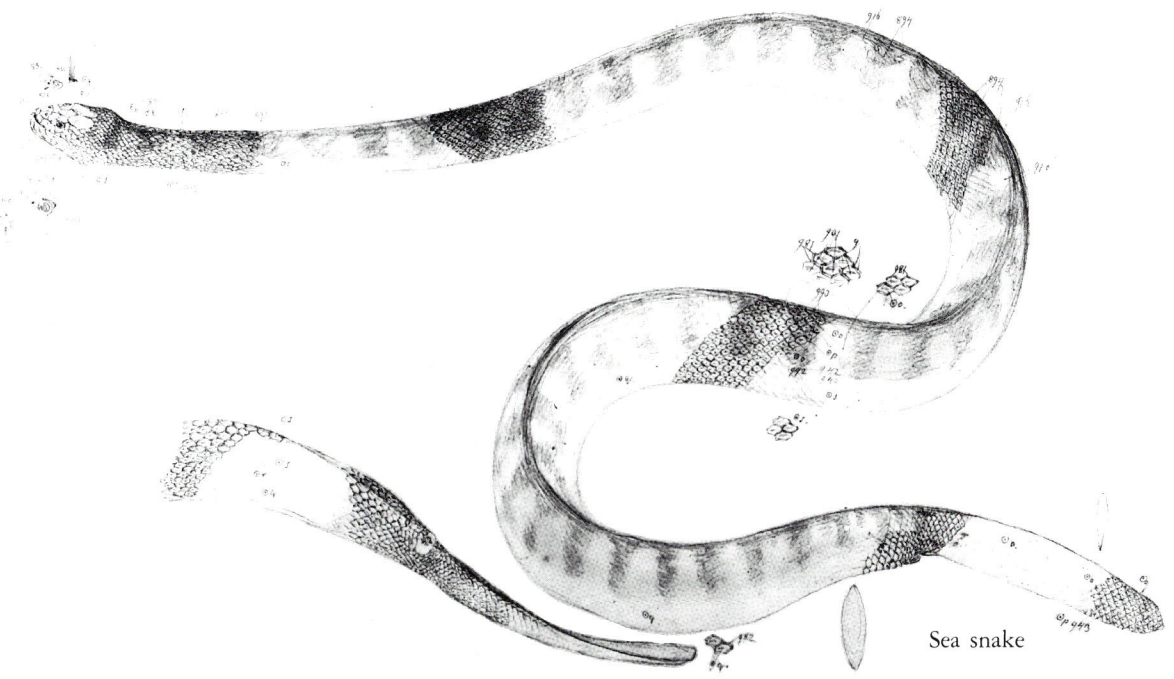

Sea snake

After landing at West Hill, Pigeon Island and Upper Head they anchored at Long Island where the ship remained from 20 to 25 September, while the scientists collected on the mainland. On 29 September they reached the Northumberland Islands and began their search for a passage through the Barrier Reef to the Coral Sea. It took them eleven days till they finally found the route today known as Flinders' Passage.

From 5 to 14 October they were, as Good describes:

in a continual labyrinth of Coral reefs Shoals and Breakers with water at times as smooth as a mill pond at other times looking like a whirlpool and such an eddy as to wheel the Ship about during which time we lost an Anchor and the Lady Nelson lost one and Broke another The Captain with some of the Gentlemen landed on one reef where they saw some singular fish and gathered some very large Shellfish . . . and a great variety of Coral.[31]

Alutera sp.

37

Glossy black cockatoo, *Calyptorhynchus lathami*

The *Investigator* then made her way back south and anchored near one of the Cumberland Islands. It was here that on 17 October Flinders made the decision to send the *Lady Nelson* back to Port Jackson and to proceed alone. The *Lady Nelson* took letters sent to England by the *Investigator's* crew including one from Ferdinand to Franz dated 18 October. After telling Franz only the barest facts he continues 'so far there have been no particular accidents except to the boat and the anchor although the coast on this side is extremely dangerous.'[32]

They left on the next day sailing further south and by the afternoon were clear of the reefs. Some of the gentlemen were seasick in the heavy swell but not Ferdinand Bauer who was surprised to find that he had such good sea legs. A week later they tried to find a passage through the breakers off Breaksea Spit near Fraser Island. Here they had another friendly encounter with the Aborigines and Good describes their canoes in great detail.

Having completed the surveying of the area, they turned back north at a fast pace and arrived at Halfway Island near Torres Strait on 30 October where Bauer, Brown and Westall made a study of the coral and collected specimens of casuarina and pandanus. They also visited Murray's Islands and three days later Bauer with Flinders and Good landed on one of the Prince of Wales Islands where they 'had a fine prospect — a number of Islands with narrow channels as much like artificial ponds & Canals as the Main Ocean'[33] but were hampered in their activities by the many bushfires. They then passed through Endeavour Strait before making their way to the Gulf of Carpentaria which they reached on 3 November.

Gulf of Carpentaria: 3.11.1802 — 11.2.1803

More than three months were spent in the Gulf of Carpentaria surveying the coasts round to Arnhem Bay. The Gulf seems to have disappointed their expectations. The country appeared monotonous, the shallow coastal water made it difficult to anchor close to the land and they only came on shore once, near the Pennefather River which Flinders mistook for the Coen River, discovered by the Dutch explorer Janssen in 1606. Of their journey south Flinders says:

> The increasing shallowness of the water made me apprehend that the Gulph
> would be found to terminate nearly as represented in the old charts, and
> disappointed the hopes found of a strait or passage leading out at some other part
> of Terra Australis.[34]

This explains a passage in Bauer's letter from Timor:

> It seems that after Captain Flinders' survey the Gulf of Carpentaria will remain as
> it appeared in the old charts with a few changes.[35]

Here Bauer sketched a myristica about which Brown wrote to Banks in March 1803: 'A species of myristica we have indeed observed differing somewhat from the specimen of m:velotina gathered by you at Endeavour River (but neither nutmeg or cocoa but native to this part of New Holland).'[36]

Since Broad Sound there had been no opportunity for re-caulking the ship and Flinders on 17 November anchored near Sweer's Island in the Wellesley Group for a thorough examination and essential repairs. The report dated 26 November was not reassuring — 'it is our joint Opinion, that in from Eight to Twelve months there will scarcely be a sound timber in her'. It only held out the faint hope that 'if she remains in fine weather and happen no accident, she may run six months longer without much Risk.'[37] Bauer gives details of the parlous state of the ship and of Flinders' quandary:

> It was found that the main part of the timbers and the side walls were completely rotten and mouldy and that the ship could not be guaranteed to last for six months on the high sea, whereupon Cap. Flinders is of a mind to head straight for Port Jackson as soon as he has finished in the Gulf.[38]

During this time there were several meetings with the Torres Strait Islanders who, according to Peter Good, resembled the Sydney Aborigines. The botanists collected avidly and brought back plants for the garden which they had set up on board the *Investigator;* though Good reports that they had problems keeping the plants alive because of the heat. On 25 November Good's entry in his journal reads: 'This day Mr. Bawer Shot a large bustard.'[39]

The scientists were pleased with their stay on the small islands clustered about the southern most point of the Gulf. 'On these Islands we made a tolerable harvest of plants — this Island contained near 200 species many of which were new'[40] On 3 December they anchored near the Bountiful Islands and went ashore on Turtle Island. 'Early a boat went ashore & came off loaded with Turtle with information the party had been very successful. Boats employed most of the day in bringing them on board & in the evening found we had 46.'[41] Here they again found the cycad:

> . . . found the Cycas circinalis in great perfection & the fruit being both pleasant to the taste and sight I eat some as also Mr Brown & Bauer. on coming on board Mr Bawer and I were taken with a violent reaching with sickness which continued with short intervals the greater part of the night."[42]

The effect on Brown seems to have been even more drastic but he did not let this interfere with his duty and identified the offending plant as *Cycas media*. This was the same plant that had had such unfortunate effects on them in King George Sound. They should have consulted the Aborigines who had long known that the seeds had to be soaked in water to leach out the poison. There is, however, no sign of resentment in Bauer's beautiful painting of *Cycas media* which was the one chosen to open the book *The Australian Flower Paintings of Ferdinand Bauer*.[43]

The next week was spent in surveying the area near Mornington Island and the Sir Edward Pellew Group of islands further west as well as the broad channels between them. On 14 December they went ashore and

> collected several fine plants found fresh water and a singular monument to the Natives. It consisted of two Stones rounded one of which was about 18 inches long the other about 1 foot and about 6 or 8 inches diameter they were fixed in the ground under the shade of Trees & well covered with bark these stones were covered with down of young birds white but in stripes & oval spots of brown or dull black.[44]

Cycad, *Cycas media*

Sea-birds

It was in this area that they found the cabbage palm (*Livistona humilis*) growing in profusion and Bauer's lovely drawing is seen here on page 44.

On 19 December they landed on Vanderlin Island, a large island near the Pellew Group where Brown and Bauer found a species of nutmeg called *Myristica insipida*. Hopes of commercial use, however, proved misplaced. That night they anchored near North Island in the Pellew Group and Peter Good comments: 'We were compleatly land locked by Islands all round us.'[45] They explored North Island for a few days while Flinders was absent surveying in the whale boat. They collected specimens, Bauer sketched a lizard and sea-birds and they found a number of fire places which showed that the island was inhabited. On Christmas Day they explored Centre Island 'but found little new.'[46]

After Flinders' return on 27 December they left 'these fine Islands which afford excellent Shelter wood & water'[47] and sailed further west. They anchored at the southern end of Maria Island on New Year's Eve and Flinders, seeing the Roper

42

Goanna, *Varanus gouldii*

River in flood, mistakenly thought that it was a tidal stream. He then proceeded to survey the west coast of the Gulf. On 4 January 1803 they explored the peninsula on the Carpentaria mainland now called Cape Barrow and found several fine plants and discovered a burial site.

> [This] consisted of poles or rather Trees hollowed by age or art & the Corps placed in the hollow of the Tree pushed in feet first at the Thick end of the Tree. which is then raised perpendicular & the Small end fixed in the ground & the Skul just in sight at the Top — Three of these poles stood together in one place & some fallen down each of which contained the Skeleton of a human body these poles were from 12 to 18 feet high, the smallest we took down & found some of the bones curiously painted with Streaks of red — five Skuls were found at the bottom of the poles well covered with bark — three other poles were found about 100 yards distant with each a skeleton — that had fallen down from age — There were some neat & large bark huts near the Standing poles.[48]

43

Cabbage palm, *Livistona humilis*

Wild nutmeg, *Myristica insipida*

Chasm Island off Groote Eylandt which they explored on 14 January provided a rich harvest of *Myristica insipida* as well as the fruit of the tree *Eugenia jambos*. Though they could not negotiate the cliffs to the very top, they were fascinated with the Aboriginal cave paintings in red and white ochre which depicted fish, turtles and kangaroos. Westall sketched these paintings as he did those on Gavern Island a few days later. Bauer's sketch of a bustard also dates from this period.

From there they returned to Cape Barrow which forms the entrance of a bay named by Flinders, Blue Mud Bay. On 20 January the first reported incident occurred involving the expedition and the local inhabitants. On Woodah Isle near the entrance of the Bay, so named because of its resemblance to a native club called a waddy or woodah, they had an altercation with the Islanders who defended their territory with spears against the *Investigator's* muskets. Flinders was surprised and troubled by this unexpected attack.

On 4 February another incident occurred which perhaps illustrates one of the early culture clashes. The expedition landed on a beach in Caledon Bay and set up its tents, when they encountered a large group of Aborigines. They seemed quite friendly but one of them made off with a hatchet belonging to Westall's servant and another snatched a musket from Brown's servant.

> Mr Bawer fired his Musket at the man who Stole the Musket but it did not take effect & we soon lost Sight of them. we then returned to the Tents & Messrs Brown & Bawer went on board with the Captain & afterwards to a point on west side of the Bay.[49]

The musket was soon returned by one of the Aborigines and on the morning of February 7 the Aborigines brought fruit, honey and some little roots to the camp which were enjoyed by the crew. They must have been quite surprised when suddenly two of them were taken hostage by the white men. Flinders thought it necessary to employ Cook's method to regain his lost hatchet.

> One was soon liberated & given to understand it was expected he would return & bring with him the Stolen hatchet which would procure liberty for the other . . . The Native was then brought on board. he expressed much anxiety when tore from his friends, on Board he was tolerable cheerful appeared sensible ate fish & bread heartily, but refused to drink Spirits, looked very attentively at every thing he saw & seemed quite confounded. on Seeing Sheep & Pigs, he took both for dogs & gave them the same name — It appears they have some knowledge of Botany and distinguish the different Trees and vegetables by distinct names.[50]

After an unsuccessful attempt to escape, the Aborigine was finally released though the hatchet was never recovered. The incident showed that while white and black men were obviously curious about each other's language and culture, they clearly had different attitudes to the concept of property.

During this time not much progress had been made in the collecting of specimens but Bauer did draw a parrot on 6 February which was later named *Psitticus brownii* (=*Platycercus venustus*), the Northern rosella or Brown's parakeet. On 11 February they weighed anchor early and passing Cape Arnhem sailed out of the Gulf of Carpentaria.

Bustard, *Eupodotis australis*

Northern rosella or Brown's parakeet, *Platycercus venustus*

Arnhem Land to Timor: 11.2.1803 — 29.3.1803

Two days later they anchored in Melville Bay and Flinders with Bauer and Westall explored caves in Gove Harbour where they found quartz crystals. On 15 February they met a large fleet of Malayan praus collecting trepang or sea cucumbers which were considered a delicacy in Chinese cooking. A brisk trade ensued and all the *Investigator's* queries about the fire places and huts they had seen were effectively answered by Pobasso, the chief of the Malayan traders. In gratitude, Flinders named an island after him.

Between 19 and 23 February they paid frequent visits to the islands that stretch 50 miles along the Arnhem Land coast and which Flinders named 'The English Company's Islands' in gratitude for the help the expedition had received from the East India Company. They then anchored in a pleasant cove off Inglis Island for four days before moving on to Arnhem Bay which Flinders named in honour of the Dutch navigators who had first discovered and named the adjoining Arnhem Land.

On 2 March Flinders and Bauer set off to survey Arnhem Bay taking provisions for a three-day excursion. They returned with a few new plants and a turtle. To Flinders' great disappointment they had not found any sign of a river. Flinders was indeed in a quandary. He wished to investigate the interesting northern coastline of Arnhem Land in greater detail, and wanted to avoid having to sail along the dangerous southern coast in winter. On the other hand the state of the ship, the ill health of the crew due to scurvy and his own lameness from scorbutic ulcers weighed heavily in the balance. His decision at this time was to end the survey of the north coast and to finish the circumnavigation of Australia as quickly as possible. His journal entry for 5 March 1803 reads: 'For Port Jackson then, we now steered away, with a fresh and fair wind.'[51] The winds, however, soon changed and prevented Flinders from following the Australian coastline. He was forced to head for Timor which in the event turned out to provide a welcome respite for the whole crew.

According to Good, 'nothing of consequence occurred' till 29 March when they saw the island of Timor. Two days later they anchored at Koepang where they were received with a 13-gun-salute and remained till 8 April. A Dutch brig under a Captain Johnson and an American vessel lay at anchor, so that they finally received news of Europe and 'all the Ships Company were refreshed with fresh provisions & fruit here & the Symptoms of Scurvey which appeared generall were soon dissipated.'[52]

Flinders, together with his officers and the scientists, called on the Governor and Captain Johnson interpreted. There is no mention of Bauer's assistance being sought, though in his letter to Franz he mentions that the Governor of Timor was a German. Bauer gives the following account of their stay in Timor:

> . . . Captain Flinders decided to go to Timor thinking that if the ship could be repaired a little it would certainly last longer on the sea and if he could get provisions in Timor for another cruise, he would like to finish the north and west coast of New Holland before going to Port Jackson . . . With regard to Natural History I have, since we left Port Jackson, made sketches of 500 species of plants but only 90 of animals, mostly birds. I have not completed anything and will not be able to do so either. The paper which I took with me on this cruise has gone mouldy because of the dampness and warmth of the cabin and is covered with spots of mould and can no longer be painted on . . . I would have written to Sir J.B. [Joseph Banks] but now I think I will leave it till we reach Port Jackson and I can see what is going to happen to the expedition once the ship Investigator has been condemned.[53]

Noisy friar-bird, *Philemon corniculatus*

From Bauer's letter it thus becomes obvious that Flinders still had not abandoned the idea of surveying the northern coast of Australia in greater detail. In a postscript hurriedly written on the envelope before their departure Bauer announces Flinders' final decision about the *Investigator's* expedition:

> Cap. Flinders has decided to go directly from Timor to Port Jackson and tomorrow, April 8, the *Investigator* will sail from here. We have received great courtesy from the Governor of Timor . . . .[54]

Flinders sent eight letters, both official and private, to England via Batavia by the Dutch brig which was in port and Brown wrote to inform Banks of their botanical survey. Bauer's letter to his brother was probably also forwarded by the same ship.

Timor to Sydney: 9.4.1803 — 9.6.1803

As instructed by the Admiralty, Flinders then surveyed the area between Timor and Trial Rocks which lay well out from the coast in the Indian Ocean. He continued south from there, as fast as the ship would allow, only coming in close to the coast again on 14 May at Cape Leeuwin and three days later in the Archipelago of the Recherche. They returned to Goose Island Bay but this time found fewer geese and no salt on Salt Island. Several of the crew died of fever and dysentery which they had probably contracted from the Koepang water. Many more, including Peter Good,

Toona australis

became gravely ill. Good's journal ends on 17 May 1803 with the following entry: 'Self and several of the Crew labouring under the Same disorder.'[55]

Flinders wanted to spend some time on further survey work but the loss of two anchors and the poor health of his men forbade it and he made for Bass Strait which he reached on 30 May. The *Investigator* sailed through Sydney Heads early in the morning on 9 June and docked near Garden Island. The Aborigine, Bungaree, rejoined his people but did make another trip with Phillip King on the *Mermaid*. Sadly, Peter Good, the gardener died on 31 May. His burial took place on 13 June from St. Phillip's Church in York Street. There was a funeral procession and three volleys were fired over the grave.

Strangely, Ferdinand Bauer does not appear to have written to his brother Franz upon their arrival in Sydney. There is, therefore, no mention of Peter Good's death nor of the funeral which we may assume he attended.

Ferdinand Bauer in Sydney: June 1803 — August 1804

On their return to Sydney, Flinders had immediately provided Governor King with the report on the *Investigator's* condition which had been prepared in the Gulf of Carpentaria the previous November. The ship was again examined and was condemned on 14 June 1803 'as unfit to proceed to sea.'[56] The crew were paid off and Flinders made arrangements for his return to England to obtain another ship. He left Sydney on 10 August 1803 but was forced to return after the wreck of the *Porpoise* on the Barrier Reef. He left Sydney again on 20 September 1803 on the *Cumberland* but because of the renewed hostilities between England and France was taken prisoner by the French in Mauritius. He was not released for six and a half years and did not reach England till 24 October 1810. At least two of Ferdinand's letters to his brother Franz which were sent with Flinders seem to have been lost as a result of these circumstances.

Brown and Bauer must have discussed the possibility of Flinders' departure for some time and had determined to remain in Australia to complete their work till Flinders' return. Brown wrote an official letter to Flinders on behalf of both of them on 13 June 1803 and received a favourable reply from Flinders four days later granting them permission to stay. Governor King's orders to Flinders regarding the crew of the *Investigator* include instructions about Bauer and Brown:

> . . . and as it has been judged conducive to forwarding the Service the Investigator was sent on, that the request of Mr. Robt. Brown, Naturalist and Mr. Ferdinand Bauer, Painter of Natural History to remain here, should be complied with to follow their respective pursuits, until it is determined whether another ship will be appointed to finish what remains of the service you had to perform; You will also discharge the above Gentlemen with their Two Servants to remain in this colony until Instructions are received from My Lords Commissioners of the Admiralty. Given etc. this 19th July 1803.[57]

White-breasted Sea eagle, *Haliaeetus leucogaster*

Brown also reported to Sir Joseph Banks in a letter sent on 6 August 1803: 'I have in conjunction with Mr. Bauer stated to him [Flinders] the advantages of our remaining here during his absence'. He goes on to announce the arrival of a letter by Bauer 'Mr Bauer who writes to you by the Porpoise will give you an account of what he has done. I can only say that he has been indefatigable and that considering the minute accuracy the number of drawings he has made is astonishing.'[58]

After putting it off for three years, Bauer finally penned his first letter to Sir Joseph on 8 August 1803. Having to write in English must have made the task even more formidable but he tries to explain the reasons for their decision to remain in Australia.

> This unexpected determination of Cap. Flinders; requierd much consideration to take such part which maight be to your departments advantageous, if an object of the Voyage we have undertaken and if such should be finished: our stay in New South Wales would add much to the collections and if not new subjects could be procurt I would be able to finish some from them wath I have already made and must bej done in England.

Grevilleae banksii

therefor our stay in New South Wales would be mor to the interest for our engagemend and has occasiond my resollution to remain here, in expectation I hope it will be approved of.[59]

Although Ferdinand did not write to Franz at this time, he did send a letter to his brother Joseph in Vienna by the same mail.

Since you received my last letter I have been in Australia or New Holland which we almost circumnavigated twice, and now the time of our absence is going to be much increased because of the ship which was found, after its second circling of this island or continent, to be unfit to leave port for a further journey. Whereupon the Commander decided to go to England and bring out another ship in order to save the voyage: we, the naturalist and I, have decided to stay in Sydney, an English colony in New Holland, and wait for the return of the Captain or till we get news from the Government which will take at least 10 or 12 months.[60]

Petalostigma quadriloculare

It is at this point in the expedition's fortunes that Jan Lhotsky's biography resumes.

Captain Flinders having decided to go back to England, Mr. Robert Brown and Mr. Bauer awaited his return in Australia; and during this period, Ferdinand visited Norfolk Island, and spent eight months there, collecting those materials from which Endlicher has been subsequently enabled to compile his Flora Norfolkica.[61]

Brown and Bauer shared a house in Sydney till the end of November 1803 when Brown decided to go to Van Diemen's Land on the *Lady Nelson* while Bauer chose to stay in Sydney. Brown was not altogether fortunate in his journey which he was later to call 'this uncomfortable expedition'.[62] It was planned to take 10 weeks and stretched to a period of nine months. He seems to have felt that Bauer had made the wiser choice. Writing to Banks in March 1804 he remarks 'pray remember me kindly to Mr. Bauer tell him I often wish for him here but at the same time could not help envying him his situation at Port Jackson . . . if there is any paper for me on board the Calcutta I beg he may use it till my return.'[63] In a later letter to Sir Joseph he writes:

Mr. Bauer did not accompany me to Van Diemen's Land which on the whole perhaps is not to be regretted as he would doubtless find ample employment here [Port Jackson.] and during last Winter was I learn uncommonly fortunate in the detection of new species of Orchideae. A very few days before my return to Sydney he embrac'd the opportunity of visiting Norfolk Island where he still remains.[64]

The orchid referred to may be the one depicted in the sketch in the Vienna collection.

After Brown's departure from Sydney, Ferdinand wrote a letter to Franz. Although he expresses satisfaction at living in 'a house in Farm Cove a mile from Sydney . . . alone and undisturbed' after the 'partnership' with Brown had ended he does sound lonely. He gently reprimands his brother for not writing; hopes that Flinders of whose misadventures he knows nothing will 'soon come out with another ship and end this voyage' and begs for news or at least rumours of what is going to happen to the expedition.[65] The letters which he mentions having sent with Flinders on the *Cumberland* do not appear to be extant and may never have reached Franz.

Together with Brown and later on his own Bauer made a number of excursions inland, as far as the Blue Mountains and the Cowpastures, to Mount Hunter and to the Grose, Nepean, Hawkesbury and George's River and as far as Newcastle 'the new settlement at the Coal or Hunters River'.[66] Bauer's sketches give a progress report of the places he visited. When Lieutenant Menzies sailed in the *Lady Nelson* on 28 March 1804 to take up his appointment as Magistrate for Newcastle he had Ferdinand Bauer on board. Menzies writing to Governor King from Newcastle on 19 April informs him:

Arr. 30 March at noon . . . Mr. Bauer will present you with a sketch of this delightful Spot, which I have taken the liberty of naming after your excellency.[67]

The original sketch appears to be lost. What has been preserved in the Mitchell Library in Sydney is a crudely coloured tracing made in the 1890s. It is labelled 'settlement of Newcastle' and shows The Nobby's before the causeway was built. This sketch is the only Australian landscape by Bauer which has come to light.

Ferdinand Bauer on Norfolk Island: August 1804 — February 1805

Finally Bauer realised that having spent several seasons in Port Jackson he had examined most of the flowers and that Brown was not coming back in the near future. He had not had any news of Flinders of whose imprisonment even the Admiralty in London knew nothing till mid-August 1804. He was aware that the *Investigator* was being patched up to enable her to make the return journey and decided to avail himself of the offer of a passage to Norfolk Island to use the remaining time to the best advantage. Captain Eber Bunker of the *Albion* had been charting the coral islands of the Bunker Group named after him during a whaling expedition in April 1803 and was now returning to England via Norfolk Island. It was he who offered to take Ferdinand there. Bauer added a postscript to the letter he sent to Sir Joseph Banks at sea on the way to Norfolk Island, 27 August 1804:

> Having heard that the produce of Norfolk Island are so different from this of New Holland, I tuk the opportunity to go with Capt. Bunker of the ship Albion, the convoyer of this letter who in his passage to England will leave me there, which will give me a time of two month to stay at the Island, when the Investigator's Ship will be finished, and come to remove the settlers with whome I shall return to Port Jackson.[68]

Like Brown he expected to be away for a short period only but had to stay for eight months because the *Investigator*, unreliable as ever, was not ready to depart. Thus

Settlement at Newcastle (*Historical Records of NSW* 5: facing p. 367, Mitchell Library, Sydney)

Brown's plans were also thwarted. He had returned to Sydney in August 1804 just after Bauer's departure and wrote to Sir Joseph Banks expressing the hope that he might spend a fortnight on Norfolk Island 'in which time I shall be able to do a good deal in so small a place.'[69]

We have no written record of Bauer's stay on Norfolk Island. He sent no letters from there and since he was on his own, there were no diary writers like Flinders, Brown and Good to report on his movements. The sketches and specimens alone bear witness to his presence on Norfolk. Using Bauer's drawings and collection, Stephan Endlicher in 1833 published the *Prodromus Florae Norfolkicae* in Vienna;

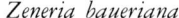

Zeneria baueriana

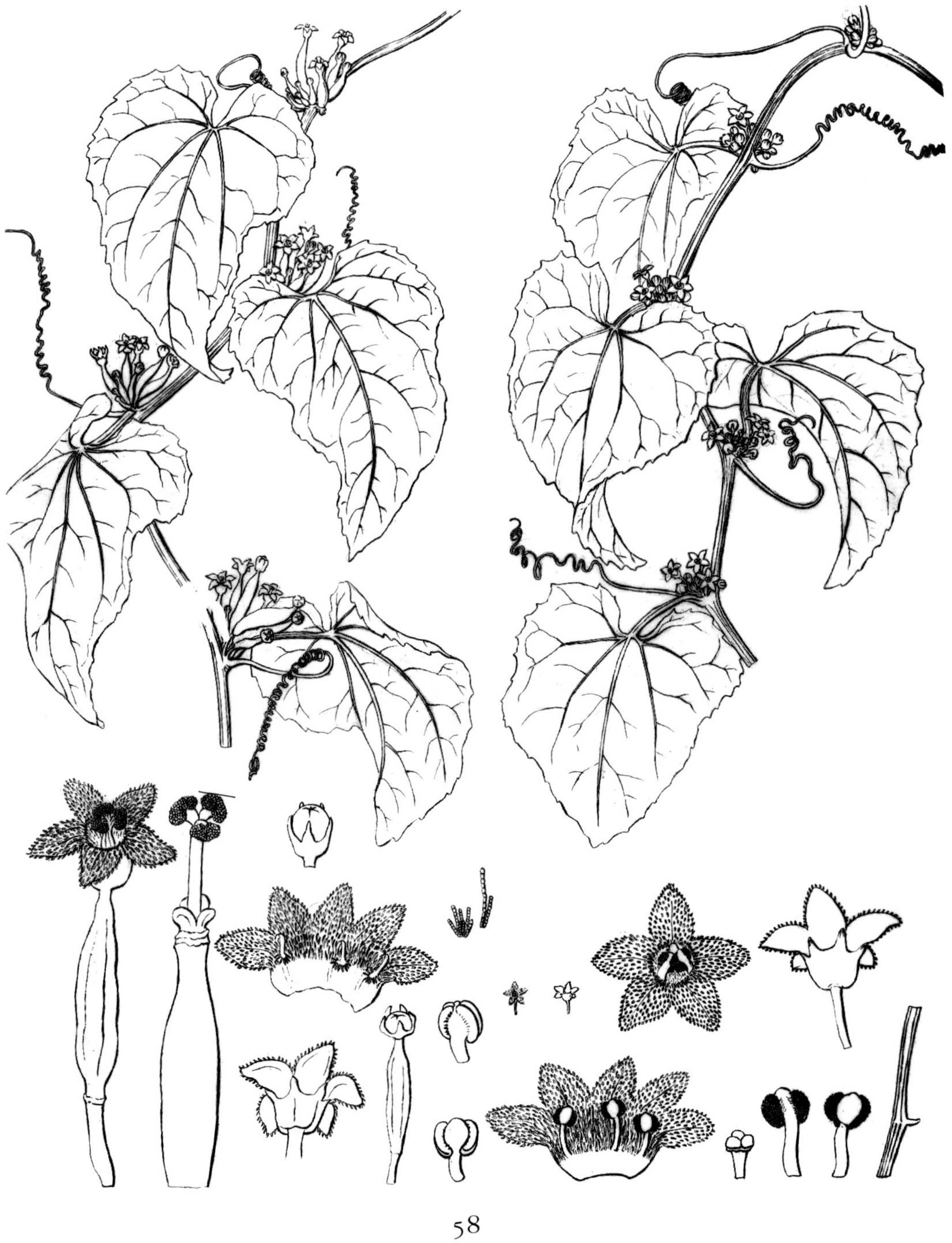

Calochilus paludosus

Phillip Island Glory Pea, *Streblorrhiza speciosa*

Bauer's illustrations appeared in the *Iconographia* which followed in 1838. Endlicher gratefully acknowledges Bauer's contribution in both title and preface:

> Whatever profit redounds to science from this small work, I believe is owed to the work of Bauer in gathering the plants, to his skill in drying them and to his clearly God-given talent in painting . . . a small volume of magnificent illustrations will shortly see the light.[70]

It is possible to trace some of Bauer's movements by the sketches and collection. He must have begun collecting as soon as he arrived since he has notes concerning the flowering season of various plants from August right through to February when he left on the *Investigator*. Amongst the 152 plants in Endlicher's catalogue are several giving a specific location such as Mount Pitt, Anson Bay, Cascade Bay, and Pig Island and Phillip Island, the last two being, in fact, the same place. Some of the collecting involved difficult walking, particularly along the coastal cliffs leading to Cascade Bay where Governor King reports finding 'woods which are of an impenetrable thickness'.[71]

A considerable number of the Norfolk Island plants were named for Bauer, for example the palm *Rhopalostykis baueri* which grows in the highest parts of the island; *Freycenetia baueriana*, a mountain rush with edible red pulpy fruit; and *Zeneria baueriana*.

In a few cases Bauer dated his sketches. *Zeneria baueriana* which flowers and bears fruit at the beginning of October was sketched on 7 October 1804; *Wickstroemia australis* which is unique to Norfolk is dated 11 September; and *Streblorrhiza speciosa* which is native to Phillip Island and flowers in October was sketched on 30 October

1804. This plant, the Phillip Island Glory Pea is, unfortunately, no longer extant since the introduction of pigs, goats and rabbits to the island (thereafter popularly known as Pig Island) destroyed its natural habitat. As the seeds are known to be capable of germinating many years after they have been collected, Professor Riedl of the Vienna Natural History Museum recently attempted to grow the plant in Schönbrunn gardens from the seeds collected by Bauer in 1804. After a promising beginning, the experiment failed but Professor Riedl intends to try again. Perhaps the seeds would regenerate more easily in their own home ground which since 1979 has been the subject of an intensive and successful land renewal programme.

There is no evidence but a strong possibility that Ferdinand Bauer may have met the first Austrian settler in Australia on Norfolk Island. Bernard Walford, an engraver, had come to Australia as a convict on the *Active* arriving on 26 September, 1791 with the third fleet of transports to New South Wales. He had been convicted to seven years' transportation for stealing a basket of laundry in Petticoat Lane, London. As an emancipist he was granted 40 acres of farming land on Norfolk and lived there from 1796 to 1805. It would seem reasonable to suppose that Bernard Walford and Ferdinand Bauer met on Norfolk Island in 1804. Walford owned land on the west coast, and Bauer, we know, explored every inch of the small island during the eight months he spent there. They would certainly have found that they had much in common: their Austrian origin; their trade as engravers; and the remarkable fate which had brought them both to a tiny island so far from home.

Bauer did not live to see his work published in Endlicher's books about Norfolk Island. According to K. A. Austin writing in 1964 only two sets — partially coloured — of Bauer's lithographs have been traced, one is in the Botany Library of the British Museum (Natural History) and the other in the Natural History Museum in Vienna.[72]

The *Investigator* eventually left Sydney on 8 January 1805 and arrived on Norfolk Island on 11 February but only stayed for a very short period. Brown writing to Banks about three weeks later comments 'Mr. Bauer has not yet returned from Norfolk Island but I expect him daily by the Investigator.'[73] She finally landed at Sydney on 3 March with the soldiers, convicts and livestock intended for Port Dalrymple and with Ferdinand Bauer on board.

After their reunion in Sydney Bauer and Brown obviously worked together for the next ten weeks. Bauer's sketches include birds and a cryptosztylis and as late as 16 May, one week before their departure, he drew a Sydney parrot.

It is important to realise that Bauer not only sketched the specimens collected by Brown but was himself a skilled and passionate collector. He had an excellent collection and his Australian plants are, today, to be found in herbaria as far apart as Capetown, Budapest and Berlin, though the bulk went to the Museum in Vienna. When the *Porpoise* was wrecked in 1803, Brown lost many of his best specimens. Although he had duplicates, these were not always of the same quality and he was grateful to Bauer for providing him with some replacements from his own collection.

The weeks before their departure were taken up with worry about the safe transportation of their collections. Brown engaged in long debates with Philip King, the Governor of New South Wales and eventually a compromise was reached

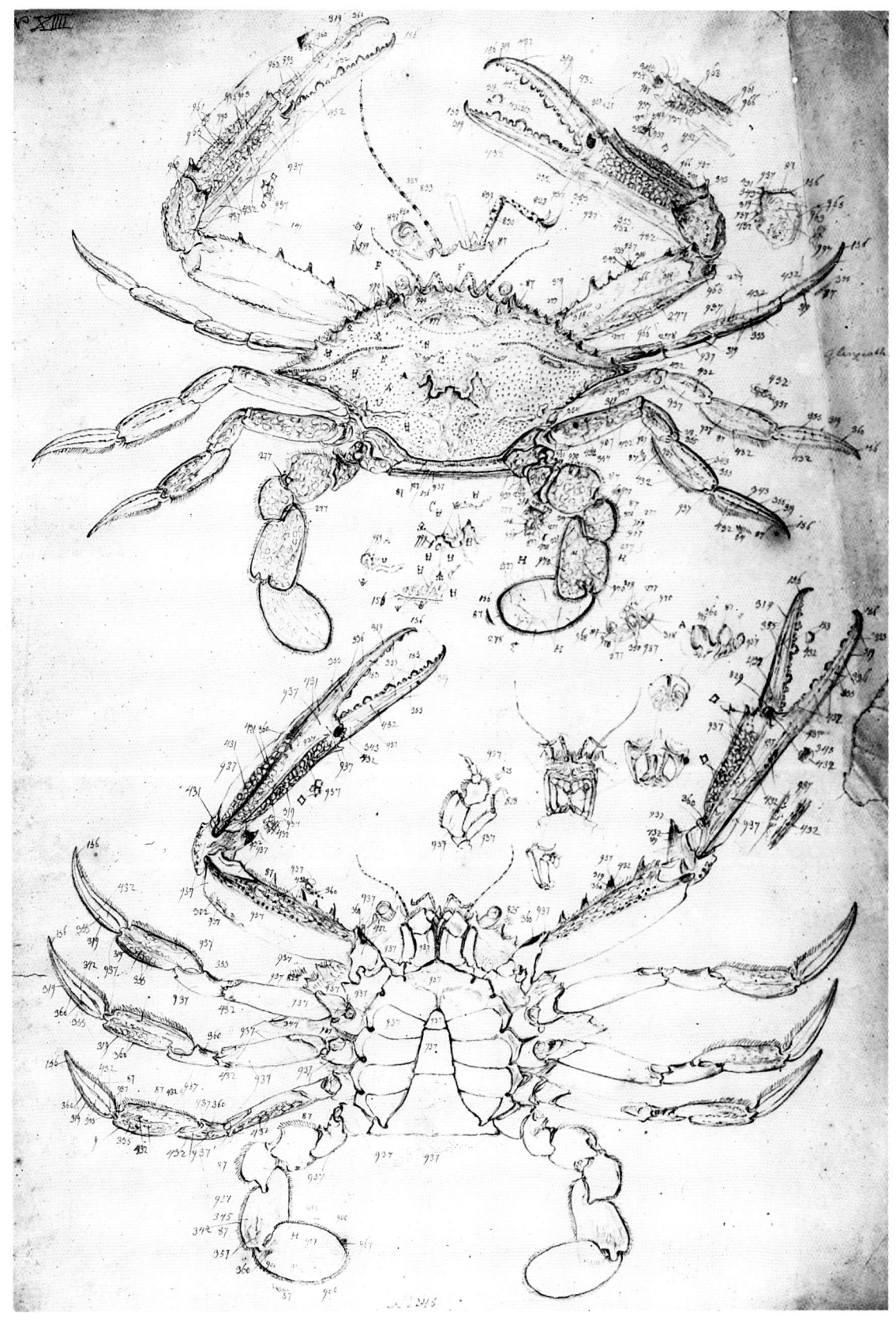

Blue swimming crab, *Portunus pelagicus*

so that the most precious part of their cargo was allowed to travel with them. Bauer's luggage amounted to 11 large cases. The stock on board included a live male wombat from the Kent Group of islands, perhaps the one collected by the scientists in 1802, which actually survived for two years in England under the tender care of Sir Everard Home, an eminent physiologist. It must have been with a sigh of relief that King wrote to Brown two months after their departure expressing the hope that his letter 'may find you, my friend Bauer and all your collection safe in London.'[74]

The *Investigator* finally left for England on 23 May 1805. The passage home on the 'crazy ship' via Cape Horn without any stops on the way was very uncomfortable but uneventful. When she finally limped into Liverpool almost five months later on 13 October Brown's and Bauer's worries were not, however, over. Getting their specimens from Liverpool to London before they all died required as much negotiating as securing their safe storage on the ship. They stayed at the Crown Inn in Liverpool while waiting for customs clearance and Brown wrote a desperate letter to Banks begging him to arrange for overland transport of the collection, rather than

Blue swimming crab, *Portunus pelagicus*

Stackhousia viminea

entrusting it once more to the tender mercies of the *Investigator* now bound for Plymouth. His fears were justified since the ship never reached Plymouth but after a disastrous journey had to put in at Falmouth. Eventually in 1810, the year that Flinders finally returned to England from his imprisonment on Mauritius, the crazy old *Investigator* was broken up at Plymouth.[75]

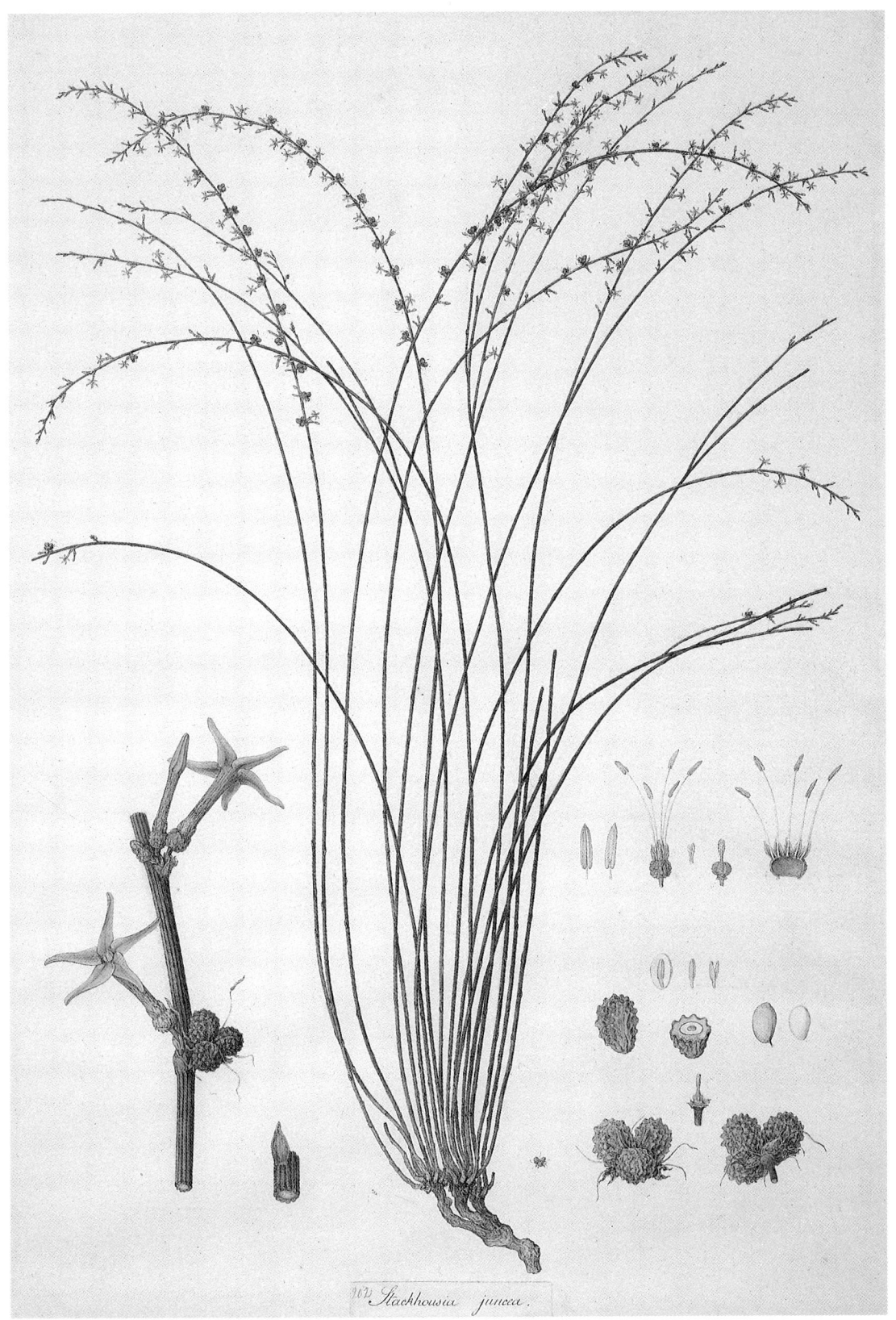

Stackhousia juncea.

Stackhousia viminea

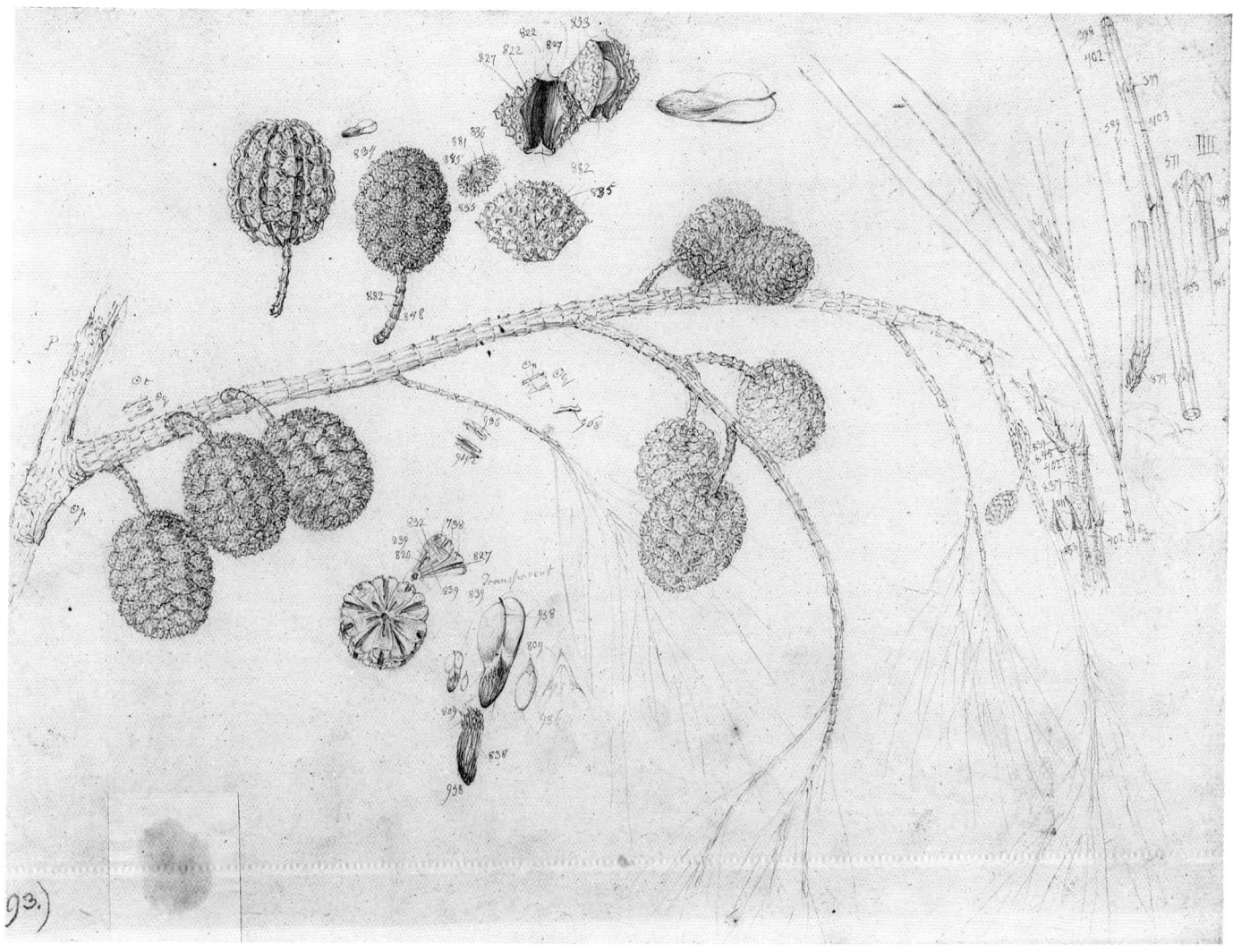

Allocasuarina tortulosa, pencil sketch & finished drawing (p. 67)

Processing the Australian Harvest

Bauer and Brown left Liverpool on 1 November and travelled to London, a city wild with excitement after Nelson's victory against the French at Trafalgar on 21 October. The naval battle overshadowed every other event. This was particularly so at the headquarters of the Admiralty where the celebrations seemed to have been even more extensive. On 5 November Bauer and Brown presented themselves there and asked for an interview with the secretary, Alexander Marsden, hoping for a sign of welcome. After waiting in vain for some three hours, they were forced to write a formal note:

66

> Robert Brown Botanist and Ferdinand Bauer Painter of Natural History
> belonging to His Majestys Ship Investigator have the honor of acquainting Mr.
> Marsden, for the information of their Lordships of their arrival in London.[76]

When Dryander, Banks' librarian, was told of their reception he was not surprised: 'The good news of yesterday would too much occupy them at the Admiralty to think of these things.'[77]

Even the arrival of the precious collection at Sir Joseph Banks' house, Soho Square, London, in November was deprived of its proper triumphal entry since Sir Joseph happened to be suffering from gout in the right arm at the time, and so could give it neither his undivided attention nor the enthusiastic admiration it deserved.

It is difficult to determine exactly how many sketches Ferdinand Bauer brought back from Australia. The figure which Lhotsky quotes in his talk but omits in the biographical sketch is clearly taken from a letter which Robert Brown wrote to Sir James Edward Smith, first President of the Linnean Society on 12 January 1806:

> Mr. Bauer whose abilities and industry you are well acquainted with, has made
> about 1600 drawings, all of them accompanied by minute dissections. In what
> manner these are to be given to the public if, indeed, we should ever have it in
> our power to publish them, it is at present impossible to say.[78]

Sir Joseph Banks in his report to Secretary Marsden sets the figure of sketches at 2073 giving a detailed analysis:

Scetches of plants made on the coasts of New Holland and New South Wales	1541
Scetches of plants made on Norfolk Island	80
Scetches of plants made on Timor	60
Scetches of plants made at the Cape of Good Hope	89
Scetches of animals made on Norfolk Island	40
Scetches of animals made on New Holland and New South Wales	263
Total Scetches	2073

Banks' account is part of a submission which he made to the Admiralty in January 1806, requesting that they retain the services of Bauer at the same salary (300 guineas) and

> that Mr. Bauer be directed to apply himself diligently to make finished drawings
> for the disposal of their Lordships of such plants or other objects of natural history
> of which he has made scetches during the voyage as shall be recommended to him
> by Mr. Brown or by me.

Banks realised that 'to finish the most interesting part only of the immense collection of scetches made by Mr. Bauer, cannot fail to be a work of considerable time' though his first estimate that it would take about three years was still wide of the mark. He undertook to

> overlook and direct the progress of these gentlemen [Brown and Bauer], to
> quicken them if they are dilatory, to assist them when it is in my power and to
> report to their Lordships the progress made by each.

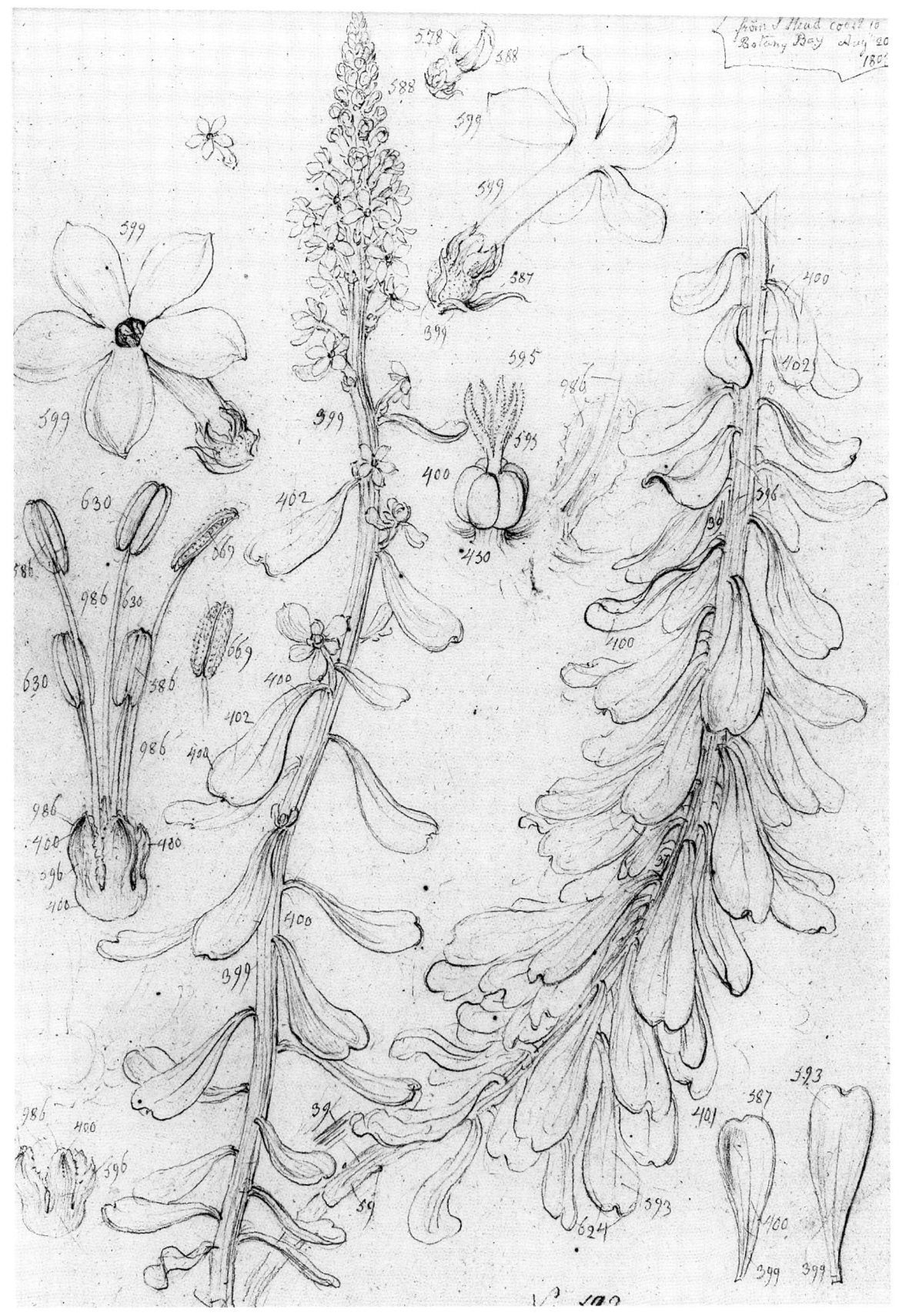

Stackhousia spathulata

Thelymitra ixioidex, pencil sketch & finished drawing (p. 71)

Platypus, *Ornithorhynchus anatinus*, pencil sketch & finished details (p. 73, *cf.*p. 109)

Banks' submission ends with the recommendation that Brown and Bauer be advised to join forces in publishing at their own expense a periodical work consisting of engravings of the Australian illustrations and their descriptions' . . . there being every reason to hope such a work will, if conducted with prudence and economy, be a source of profit to these gentlemen, as long as they are able to supply new subjects, either beautiful to the eye or interesting to science.' Banks enclosed an example of Bauer's art with his submission. It is of 'a very curious and interesting plant found by our travellers at King George's Sound.'[79] Unfortunately, the plant was not found with the manuscript and so has never been identified.

The plants from Brown's collection and Bauer's sketches had originally been left at the house of Sir Joseph but Bauer soon removed his sketches to his own house in order to continue working on them. Bauer produced around 300 magnificent water colours of his Australian sketches, each a complete masterpiece. The colour code using up to four figures which he had devised for his sketches allowed him to reproduce the finest nuances of colour with absolute accuracy so that Sir Joseph Banks marvelled: 'It is beyond what, I confess, I thought it possible to perform.'[80] He and Brown were still working on the Australian collection when Flinders arrived back in London in 1810.

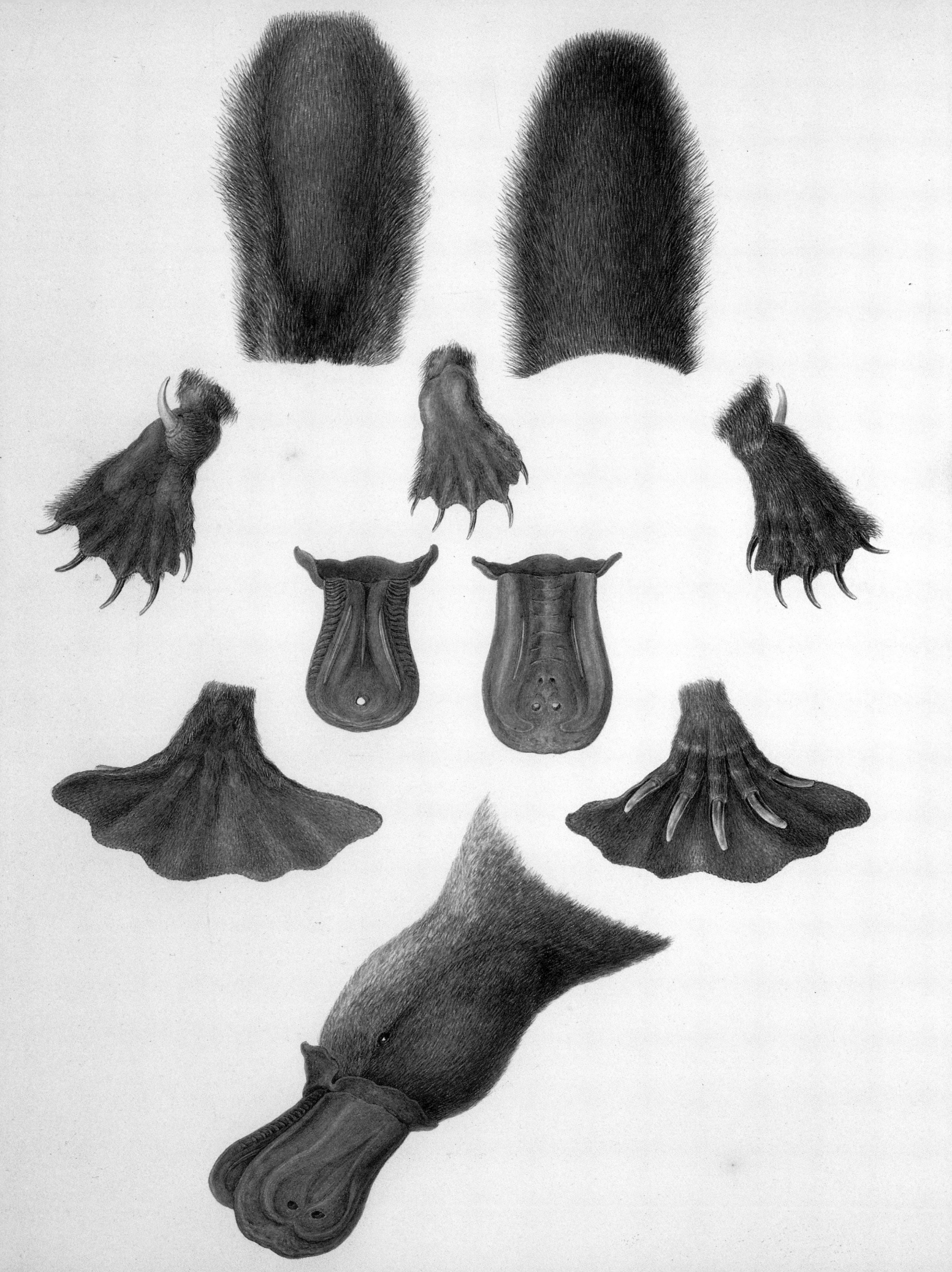

Flinders arrived at Spithead on Wednesday 24 October 1810 and made straight for London by coach where he put up at the Norfolk Hotel. Here he celebrated a touching reunion with his wife, Ann, and went on the same day to the Admiralty to get news of his promotion and his future prospects. On the way back to the hotel after a satisfactory interview with the First Lord of the Admiralty

> Flinders met Ferdinand Bauer in the street, and their reunion was both cordial and joyful. Later that evening, Robert Brown called at the hotel, having heard the news from Bauer and again there was a long recital of events since their parting at Sydney in 1803. When Brown had left, Ann and Matthew were, at last, alone.[81]

> *Although considerable delay took place ere Flinders' voyage was published, still its intrinsic and geographical value was duly appreciated. Bauer bore his full share in contributing to the production on this work, and I incline to think that he assisted Mr. Westall in executing the landscapes for I know of no book . . . where plants and groups of foreign trees, Seaforthea, Xanthorrhaea and Casuarina, are pourtrayed with such surpassing beauty and truth. In the appendix, the description of ten species of plants are from Mr. Brown; these had been selected out of 'the invaluable collection of drawings made by Bauer'. It is easy to perceive by a glance at these plates that they were never executed at home, and from dried specimens. Figures of* Flindersia australis, Eudesmia tetragona, *and* Franklandia fucifolia, *are acknowledged by botanists to surpass every thing of the same kind.*[82]

Flinders spent the next four years getting his monumental work *A Voyage to Terra Australis* ready for publication. It comprised two quarto volumes of text illustrated with nine engravings by William Westall and a folio atlas. Volume 2 included an 80-page appendix on the *Botany of Terra Australis* written by Brown, while the atlas consisted of charts, four coastal views by Westall and ten unnumbered plates of botanical specimens by Bauer to illustrate Brown's botanical appendix. The three volumes were published by G. & W. Nicol and appeared on 18 July 1814, a day before its author died.

Jonathan Wantrup considers Flinders' Voyage 'the most outstanding work on the coastal exploration of Australia'. In 1985 a deluxe copy which included the folio atlas sold in Sydney for $15 750.[83]

Robert Brown had already published the first volume of his *Prodromus Florae Novae Hollandiae et Insulae Van-Diemen* in 1810. It was an octavo volume written in Latin without any illustrations. Since only 26 copies of the 250 published were ever sold, no second volume appeared but in 1830 Brown published a 40-page supplement entitled *Supplementum primum Prodromi Florae Novae Hollandiae*.

> *In the year 1813, Bauer began his* Illustrationes Florae novae Hollandiae; *a work which did not meet with the encouragement it deserved. The cause of failure lay wholly with our author himself; but the error which he committed was of the most honourable kind; for it may be truly said that this publication outstripped, by at least a score of years, the capacities and attainments of the time at which it appeared. There is something very naive in the remark made on the subject in a letter written by Bauer's brother. He says, 'Ferdinand could not find people capable either of engraving or colouring the plates properly,*

Crow's ash, *Flindersia australis*

and he was consequently obliged to execute every part of the work with his own hands, thus occupying far too much time. Very few, indeed, coloured copies has he been able to prepare and sell'. Thus a botanical book which would have been appreciated and supported in the year 1834, or even during the magnificent and art-encouraging reign of Napoleon in France, fell to the ground in 1814.[84]

Lhotsky's comment on the cause of the failure, which he obviously meant as a back-handed compliment, has been taken literally by later biographers, and Bauer's perfectionism and determination to do the whole work himself are seen as the cause of the financial failure and subsequent abandonment of the project. But blaming Bauer's high standards for the failure of the publishing venture seems to me a misreading of the situation. After all, as Lhotsky himself quite rightly states, the period during the Napoleonic Wars was, for a variety of political and artistic reasons, a particularly bad time for launching expensive botanical publications. The volumes by Flinders and Brown suffered the same unhappy fate as, indeed, did Sir Joseph Banks' own *Florilegium.* A letter written by Franz Bauer to his friend Joseph von Jacquin in September 1814 (of which unfortunately a vital page is missing) confirms what we know of the difficult circumstances.

My situation and occupation is much the same it has been for so many years. Of the *Kew Plants* are only three numbers published; the work being on too large a scale, and requiring too much labour, it could not be sold but with considerable loss, and my engraver diing, the work was dropt near twelve years ago. Since that time I received from Sir Joseph Banks an annual Salary, and all the Drawings I make, are his property. I have lately finished a very interesting work to which I gave the title of *Illustrations of the Germination and Vegetation of the Wheat, and the several Diseases of Corn.* I was near seven years occupied with that work: Sir Joseph wished to have it published, but we cannot find any engraver here to execute the plates. At present I am Chiefly occupied with the Orchiteous plants, of which I have a considerable number, and which would make a most interesting work; however I have very little hopes of ever seeing any of my performances published here.

If Franz, with all Sir Joseph's support behind him could not find an engraver for his work how much more hopeless was his brother's case, with no financial backing of any kind.

Franz continues:

My Brother after whom You kindly inquire, since his return from his Voyage to *Terra Australis*, was about six years employed by the Admiralty, to make finished Drawings of the most interesting Plants from that part of the World; those Drawings are now deposited in the Library of the Admiralty, where nobody ever can see them again. Since the completion of that engagement my Brother begun a most excellent work on his own account, from the Sketches an [sic] Herbarium which he made and collected during his Voyage and which are now his own property; under the following title — *Ferdinand Bauer Illustrationes Florae Novae Hollandiae, sive Icones Generum quae in Prodromo Florae Novae Hollandiae et Insulae Van Dimen {sic} descripsit Robertus Brown.* This work is the size of the Hortus Schönbq; drawn, engraved and colord in a highly finished style, by himself: it appears in numbers of five plates, at one Guinea and a half p^r number the colord, and at five Shillings p[r] number the plain — there are already two numbers published, but though the work is highly approved off, the sell of it here is so inconsiderable that my Brother could not clear the fiveth part of his expenses; he therefore determined to leave England and packet up his whole collection of Drawings, consisting of more 2000 of plants, several hundrets of animals, Birds, Fishes, Snakes etc etc also his [the following page is unfortunately missing, but from other sources one may assume that the end of the sentence read: also his valuable herbarium and collection of skins].[85]

Ferdinand published only three parts of what was intended to be a much larger work to accompany Brown's *Prodromus* and so provide, as Sir Joseph Banks had hoped, a comprehensive survey in text and illustration of the botany of Australia. The three parts which were published in less than 50 copies contained 15 exquisite, large folio plates. They were available, as Ferdinand states on the cover, directly from the author at '10, Russel-street, Bloomsbury'.

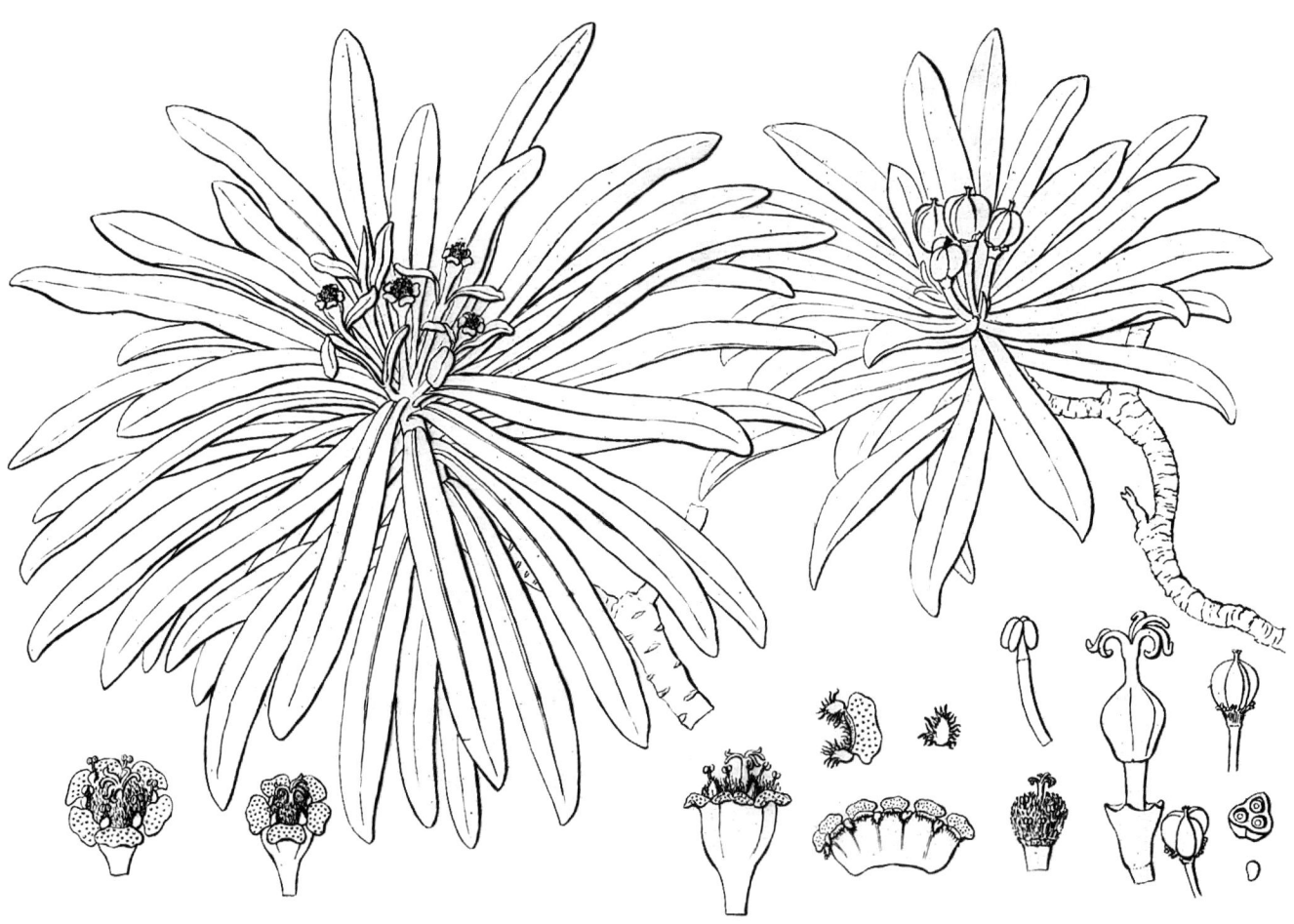

Euphorbia glauca

Macrotropis formosa.
Bossiaea dentata

Blue pincushion, *Brunonia australis*

The date of publication is given as 1813 but the first fascicle or part appeared in 1806 and the last after 1814. This is confirmed in the letter by Franz quoted above and by a letter dated 2 January 1817 which Joseph von Jacquin wrote to A.P. de Candolle where he mentioned the recent publication of the third fascicle.[86]

A few copies including that held by the British Museum contain a 16th plate depicting the *Lambertia formosa*. A letter which Stephan Endlicher wrote to George Bentham on 12 May 1833 indicates that Endlicher bought the unsold copies of the plates from Bauer's estate and that they were then dispersed.[87]

It would surely have amazed Bauer to know that in 1982 a coloured copy of his *Illustrationes* sold for $US25 000.[88]

Pomaderris myrtilloides

Return to Austria

It appears, from documents in my possession, that Ferdinand was excessively and unduly disheartened by this failure; so much so, that, fearing he should never be able to do anything else; he gathered up his papers, and closing, as it were, his accounts and transactions with the literary and scientific world, determined to withdraw to his native land, taking with him his most extensive collections, drawings of more than 2000 species of plants, several hundred sketches of animals, a very valuable herbarium and collections of skins, the whole occupying fourteen large cases, with which he set sail from England in August 1814.

The liberality with which Ferdinand Bauer had been treated by the English government, in whose service he had remained finishing the plates illustrative of the expedition, up to the year 1813, enabled him, on his return to Austria, to purchase a small house at Hitzing, near Vienna, adjacent to the large Botanic Garden of Schoenbrunn. Here he worked very hard in executing and completing his drawings of New Holland plants and animals, as well as some plates of his Illustrationes, *filling two large volumes with the former. He enjoyed the friendship of the different Naturalists in Vienna.[1]*

Unfortunately, it has not been possible to trace the documents which Lhotsky quotes as his source for Ferdinand's emotional state. One can only wonder whether Ferdinand, quite uncharacteristically, unburdened himself in letters to friends in England or to relatives in Austria or whether others, in close contact with him at the time, reported on his deep depression.

Most biographies whether written in English or in German use Lhotsky's article as their sole reference for this period and are therefore very similar in their accounts, though the Austrian ones do tend to explain his return to his native land as motivated by patriotism or homesickness rather than by commercial failure.

As if in compensation for this gap in psychological knowledge, researchers' luck has proved kind in at least allowing me access to other documents which reveal something about the contents of those '14 large cases' which accompanied Ferdinand when he left England in August 1814. It was with little hope of success that I approached the archivists in the Vienna Town Hall with the request for information about Austria's most forgotten artist. Hietzing, where Bauer had died, is now a suburb of Vienna but this was not the case in 1826. To my great surprise — and that of the archivist — a large file with documents relating to Ferdinand Lucas Bauer was instantly located in the catalogue and had, by the next day, emerged from the repository. It contained his last will and testament; a detailed inventory and official valuer's report of his assets in money, property, furnishings and other valuables; as well as a catalogue of his personal library and various correspondence relating to the execution of his will, including two letters from Franz Bauer.

For the Austrian bureaucracy of the time, the significant feature about Ferdinand Bauer was not his international fame as a botanic artist, but the fact that he was a house owner. The term 'Hausbesitzer' accompanies almost every mention of his name. His house was, moreover, located in Hietzing, the elegant district where the palace of Schönbrunn is to be found. According to the will, the address was Schmidgasse 155 and the house was situated at the corner of Schmidgasse and Gloriettegasse. Today, Schmidgasse is called Trautmannsdorfgasse but the place, where Bauer's house stood, is now designated Gloriettegasse 12. The house which has replaced his smaller cottage is a very grand villa dating from the 1880s. It is surrounded by many tall trees, some of which may well have been planted by Ferdinand himself. Standing on that corner, one immediately realises that what made the site particularly attractive to Ferdinand was the fact that it was but a stone's throw from the Botanical section of the Imperial and Royal Gardens of Schönbrunn. The location of Ferdinand's house thus presents a strange mirror image of that which Franz, living in England, chose for his home next to the Royal Botanic Gardens in Kew.

Ferdinand's house which together with a garden was valued at 3000 florins must have been quite substantial and the inventory suggests that it was well appointed and comfortably furnished. The furniture was of polished walnut, and the dining room had a large table with matching chairs upholstered in velvet. A picture in a golden frame hung on one wall probably in the sitting room just above the sofa which stood surrounded by five upholstered cherrywood chairs. There were two clocks, a mirror, a portrait and a profusion of small tables, chests, boxes and suitcases.

The contents of Ferdinand's wardrobe suggest that he did not live a hermit's life. He owned tails for state occasions, a frock coat, an overcoat, eight waist coats and a considerable number of shirts and trousers. He was also well equipped for his mountain excursions with three pairs of boots, a pair of lederhosen and two umbrellas. On retiring to bed he wore a night shirt and one of his four night caps.

The small amount of cutlery found in the inventory suggests that Ferdinand, a confirmed bachelor, was not in the habit of inviting many friends to dine with him but preferred more intimate gatherings for 'Jause' (Viennese afternoon tea) when the silver coffee spoons came into their own.

If the conversation flagged Bauer's guests certainly had enough to look at. The inventory shows a substantial library of over 100 titles, many in several volumes, ranging from dictionaries in German, English, French, Latin, Italian and Czech to standard natural history reference books, his own works and those of his friends, art books, English and French literature and a book on becoming a master at chess. His own Australian illustrations filled two volumes and were bound in red morocco leather. Most in evidence, however, was his collection of botanical, geological and zoological specimens. There were Brazilian and Australian butterflies, shells, mooses' heads and the Australian waddy which he had found on the Mornington Peninsula in 1802. When all else failed Ferdinand could provide entertainment by demonstrating his camera clara and obscura — at least the inventory lists the curtain used for these performances. One room was probably set aside for his painting. Here stood special tables for drawing as well as a variety of the tools of his trade such as three compasses, a microscope, paints and drawing instruments. There were also several cupboards filled with over 2000 sketches.

In 1819, Bauer again visited England in order to see his brother, and the other valued friends, with whom a companionship of nearly 30 years had quite assimilated his ideas and feelings. He soon afterwards returned to Vienna, and continued to devote himself closely to painting most of his production being destined to go to England, where, besides the works mentioned above, were published his plates for the late Mr. A.B. Lambert's work on Pinus, *Lindley's* Digitalis, *& c.*

Thus continually engaged in the furtherance of his cherished science, and undertaking, even at this advanced period of life, botanical excursions into the Alps of Austria and Styria, and making collections of the plants which he there found, Bauer was seized, in the year 1825, by illness, which terminated his existence on the 17th of March, 1826, in the 66th year of his age. The bulk of his collections was bequeathed to his legal heirs; but the two volumes of miniature paintings of Australian plants and animals, he left to his brother Francis, by whom they have been recently sold to Mr. Robert Brown. His herbarium and skins of animals and birds, with the sketches illustrative of them were purchased for the Imperial Museum of Vienna, and a great many drawings, as well as copies of the Illustrationes, *were still, in the year 1829, in the possession of his brother Francis at Vienna.* [2]

Ferdinand's herbarium and natural history collection was obviously well known and highly regarded in scientific circles, since no lesser person than Leopold Trattinick, the Keeper of the Kaiserliches Naturaliencabinet (the forerunner of the Natural History Museum in Vienna) was asked to be a valuer of Ferdinand's estate and signed the inventory. There have been many varying estimates made of the total number of Australian drawings which Bauer left. The figure most often quoted is that of 2073 mentioned by Sir Joseph Banks in his submission to the Admiralty in January, 1806. Another figure of 1542 sketches of New Holland and 60 of Norfolk Island is taken from a list compiled by Bauer which is preserved in the British Museum (Natural History). The list may have been enclosed in a letter which, according to Maiden, Bauer wrote to Banks. The list in Bauer's hand is headed:

Native-cat, *Dasyurus* sp.

List of Sketches
     of
Plants and Animals
   made during
the Voyage of his Majesties Ship Investigator
and subsequently
at Port Jackson & Norfolk Island
     by
Ferdinand Bauer

It is divided into the flora and fauna of the Cape of Good Hope; New Holland and Norfolk Island. The flora is then further divided according to the Linnean classification while the fauna is classified as animals, birds, amphibia, fish and insects.[3]

The inventory, unfortunately, does not really clarify the issue. It mentions one chest with drawings and sketches of New Holland valued at 24 Florin; one collection of drawings valued at 40 Florin; and one exercise book with 16 drawings of Greece worth 16 Florin. The two books of animal and plant drawings bound in morocco, containing an unspecified number of Australian water colours were not valued and were, as Lhotsky states, bequeathed to his brother Franz. The will also stipulates that his copy of the *Illustrationes* and the unpublished engravings together with all the rest of his sketches are to be auctioned. We know that Endlicher acquired his coloured engravings at this time.

It would appear that of the 252 water colours of Australian plants, representing 236 species, which Bauer completed in England, 203 belonged to the Admiralty by the terms of his contract. They were bequeathed by the Lords Commissioners to the British Museum in 1843. Bauer took 49 with him to Vienna and these were among the ones which were left to Franz and eventually sold to Brown. Brown then also bequeathed them to the British Museum in 1858.

Bauer seems to have died on the night of 17 March for his death is recorded in the register of the Parish Church of 'Maria Geburt' in Hietzing on this date, while it is given as 18 March in the official documents held by Vienna Town Hall. He received the last sacraments and was buried according to the rites of the Catholic Church and, as he had stipulated in his will, six masses were said for the repose of his soul.

Koala, *Phascolarctos cinereus*

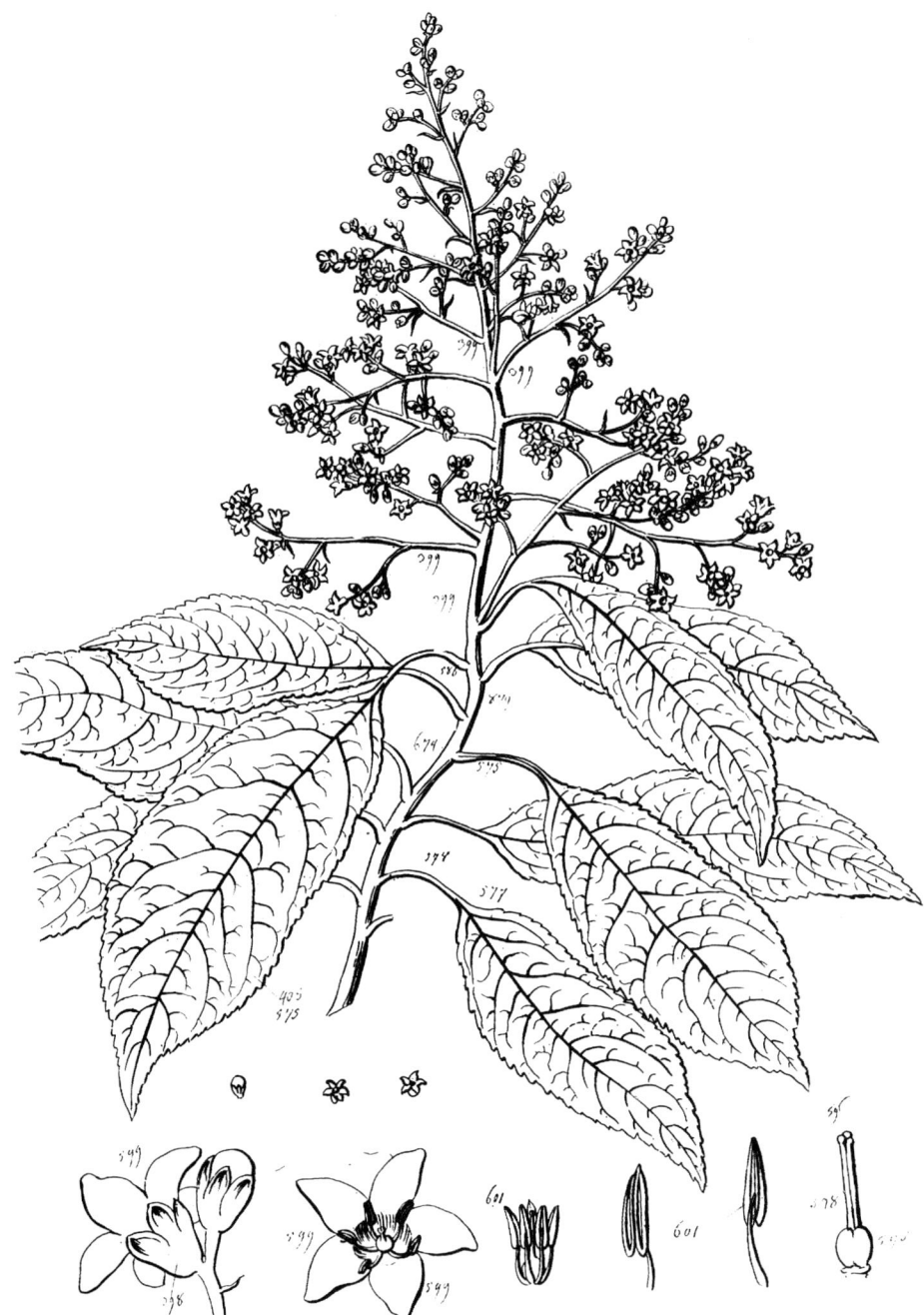

Ehretia acuminata

The funeral took place on 19 March and he appears to have been buried in the churchyard. A notice of Ferdinand's death appeared in the botanical journal *Flora:*

> Am 17. März starb zu Wien an der Wassersucht und Gicht der verdiente treffliche Pflanzenmaler Ferd Bauer, Begleiter R. Brown's, dem zu Ehren bekanntlich eine Bauera gebildet wurde.

> (On 17 March the death occurred in Vienna from dropsy and gout of the meritorious, most excellent botanical artist Ferd Bauer, who accompanied R. Brown and who had, as is well known, the Bauera named in his honour).[4]

A year later the same journal announced the sale of the herbarium to the Austrian Imperial Botanic Museum.

> The herbarium belonging to the deceased botanical artist Ferdinand Bauer who as is well known was in New Holland with R. Brown has been bought by the Imperial Botanical Museum for a price of 1500 fl C.M. It contains in addition to many plants of the flora of New Holland which have never been described, many original drawings which considerably increase its value.[5]

This explains why Bauer's collection is today split between the British Museum (Natural History) and the Natural History Museum in Vienna. While most of the water colours are held in London, the black and white sketches which preceeded them are to be found in Vienna. Until fairly recently these were kept in the herbarium together with the seeds and dried specimens which were often attached to them. Today they are housed separately and are presently being restored. Austria has altogether about 1800 sketches of Australian plants, 100 Norfolk Island plants, 150 Timor and Cape of Good Hope plants and 100 of animals. There are also 4 water colours of Norfolk Island plants, one of which, the *Wickstroemia australis*, is here reproduced for the first time in colour.

After Franz Bauer's death in 1840, 20 lots of Ferdinand's drawings again came up for auction, this time in London. Many of these were acquired by Ernst August, the Duke of Cumberland and a friend of Franz Bauer's, who in 1837 had become King of Hannover. Together with many volumes of paintings by Franz Bauer, Ferdinand's Greek and Turkish views were presented to the Library in the University of Göttingen where they are still to be found today.

Bearded dragon, *Amphibolurus barbatus*

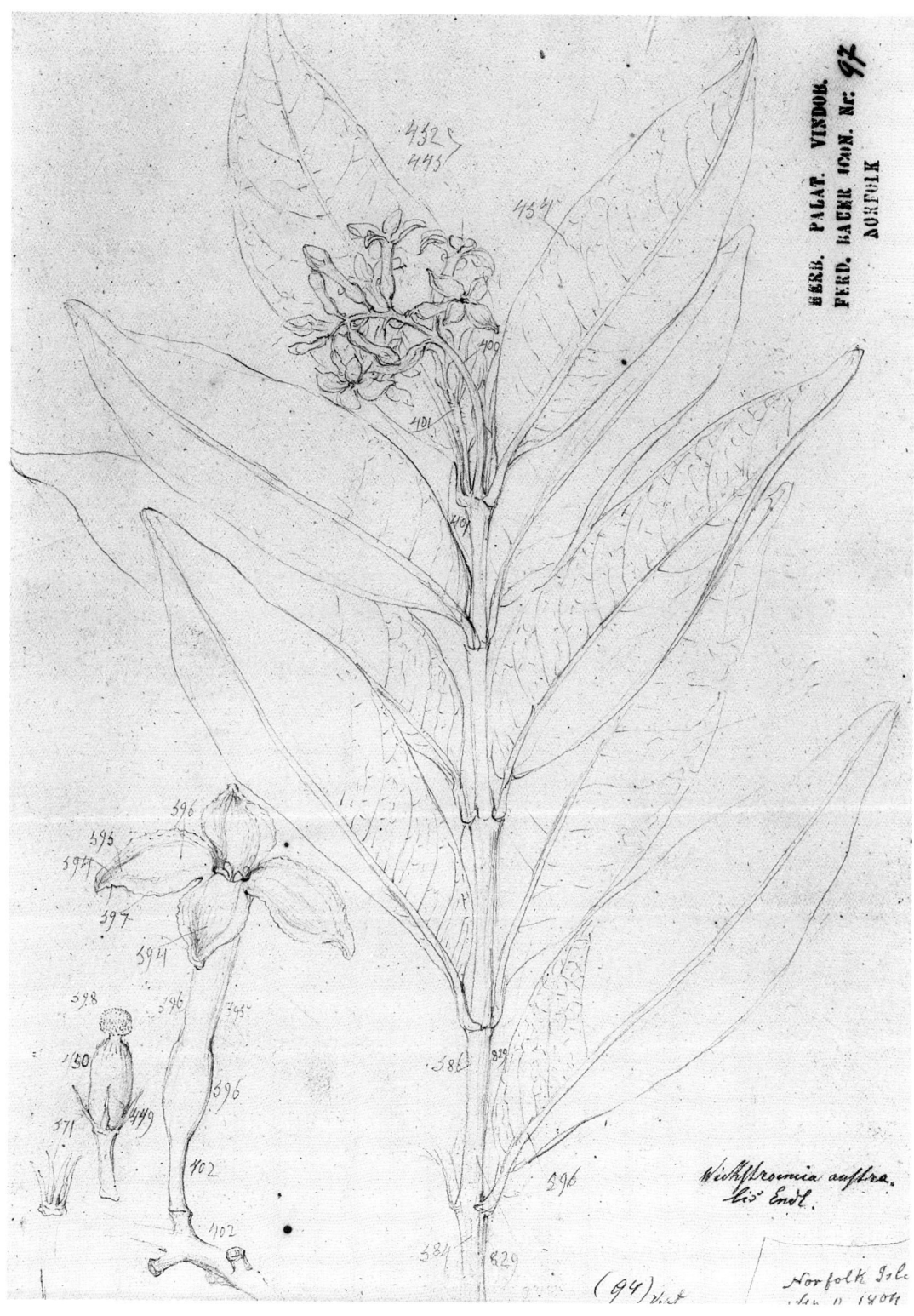

Wickstroemia australis, pencil sketch & finished drawing (p. 89)

Wickstroemia australis Endl.

The Indefatigable Mr Bauer

Ferdinand Bauer, as his conduct through life proved him and his private letters attest, was a plain straightforward man, full of application and energy. His temper was most kind, and hardly had he obtained his appointment in the 'Investigator', than he hastened to aid most liberally some of his indigent relations. He ever preserved a deep sense of gratitude towards those friends and patrons, who had done him service . . . His own name, recorded as it is by his superior botanical designs, commemorated by the genus Bauera in the annals of botany, and, as we before stated, in those also of geography, will long live in the recollection of posterity.[1]

Lhotsky concludes his account of Ferinand Bauer with a fine testimonial to his worth as a human being. Though he never met Ferdinand, what he says of his personal qualities — his industry, gentleness and generosity — is certainly born out in the comments of those who knew him, above all those who shared the arduous Australian voyage. Further corroboration can be found in the letters and published writings of the scientists with whom he collaborated and in the pages of his last will and testament where he remembers his relatives, friends and servants.

His 'application and energy' seem to have impressed everyone. He was so committed to his work that he appeared impervious to physical hardship, illness, danger and the social life going on around him. Unlike Brown, who frequently complains of being incapable of working because of ill-health, Bauer is always at pains to reassure his brother that he is in the best of health; unlike Flinders who tells Ann interesting details about life on board the *Investigator*, Bauer only mentions Flinders and Brown by name and does not make a single personal comment about anyone during his five years in Australia.

It is probably the combination of single-minded concentration and constant effort which is expressed by the term 'indefatigable', an adjective which accompanies Ferdinand like the standing epithets in Homer's *Odyssey*. Thus, when Brown refers to Bauer as 'indefatigable' in his letters to Banks in May 1802 and August 1803, the latter responds in kind by sending his best wishes 'for all success in his meritorious labors to Mr. Bouer [sic] who I know is indefatigable.'[2]

Besides his conscientiousness, the quality that is most often highlighted is his gentleness and amiability. One has the feeling that he fitted, to an unusual degree, the job description which the Admiralty wrote for the 'gentlemen of science' on the *Investigator* expedition. The agreement to which Bauer and his colleagues put their names 'on 29 April, in the year of our Lord, 1801' stipulated that they were

to conduct themselves peacably quietly and civily to each other, each readily
assisting the other in his respective department, to the utmost of his ability, in
such manner as will best promote the success of the public service in which they
are jointly engaged, and unite their individual endeavours with one general result
. . . all deviations from good humour and perfect harmony among the parties [are
to be] punished.[3]

Flinders in his private journal as well as in his official reports finds that Bauer fulfils
all his expectations as a pleasant travelling companion. It is, therefore, particularly
interesting to come upon an uncomplimentary reference to Bauer which he made in
the draft of a letter to Ann but crossed out and did not include in the actual letter,
perhaps feeling that it was rather too severe. The letter was drafted on 25 June 1803
in Sydney upon the completion of the voyage but was not sent until 13 July 1804
when Flinders was imprisoned on Mauritius. It describes his relationship with the
officers and scientists on the *Investigator*. The remarks which were crossed out by
Flinders are here given in brackets.

Mr. Brown is recovered from ill health and lameness (we are not altogether
cordial, but our mutual anxiety to forward far the complete success of the voyage
is a bond of union; he is a man of abilities and knowledge, but wants feeling
kindness). Mr. Bauer, your favourite, is still polite and gentle (and is so to a
considerable depth but I fear there is a dreadful disposition at the bottom). Mr.
Westall wants prudence, but he is good-natured: The last two are well and have
always remained upon good terms with me. Mr. Bell is misanthropic, and pleases
nobody (he may possibly leave us) . . . Trim, like his master, is becoming grey.[4]

Perhaps the dramatic comment about Bauer refers to an incident mentioned by
Wilfrid Blunt:

Ferdinand's industry was colossal and he seems to have remained unperturbed by
the dangers and hazards of the long voyage. Only once — when the water poured
into his cabin and destroyed a number of his drawings — do we hear of his
temper being overtaxed.[5]

Flinders may have discovered the limits of Bauer's amiability. Perhaps his polite-
ness was in a way designed to keep people at a manageable distance in order to
preserve his working time. The social controls only failed when his work was
threatened.

   In the absence of a portrait, it is tempting to use a literary source for further
insight into Ferdinand Bauer's personality. It may come as a surprise to many that
our unknown artist actually figured in a well-known Australian historical novel.
Ernestine Hill whose thoroughly researched book, *My Love Must Wait*, introduced
Matthew and Ann Flinders to a generation experiencing the misery of war-time
separation, gives Bauer a minor role in her story. She mentions him five times in all
and, having only Flinders' diaries and letterbooks to provide information, has to
look elsewhere for additional material. Her own experiences of Austrians, and
indeed of any 'foreigners', were no doubt rather limited and, or so it seems to me,
she therefore turned to the cinema for her inspiration. Ernestine Hill's Ferdinand
Bauer character is vaguely reminiscent of Szakal, the Hungarian star who used to
portray kindly but ridiculous Germans in films of the 40s and 50s. Bauer is said to

be 'clumsy' while 'exuding geniality and enthusiasms' as he sits 'beaming behind his spectacles'. His sensitive paintings are said to be the work of clumsy fingers. In the final chapter entitled. *The Dead awakes*, the historian takes over from the novelist as Ernestine Hill comments: 'Of his men of the *Investigator*, three attained transcendent fame, Robert Brown, greatest of English botanist, Charles Westall, R.A.; and Sir John Franklin' — she is of course perfectly correct for at this stage there was no sign of Bauer 'awakening from the dead'.

There is no factual evidence for either Bauer's clumsiness or his short-sightedness and one might disregard Ernestine Hill's sketch of Bauer as a poor likeness meant only to fill in the background of her novel, were it not for her phrase 'clumsy Bauer's delicate penmanship'[6] which seems to reveal her intuitive grasp of a basic discrepancy. She is, I would suggest, reacting to the fundamental incongruity of an imperfect human being producing a perfect work of art. It will be remembered that the same insoluble riddle plagues Salieri in Peter Shaffer's play *Amadeus* which deals with Mozart as a fallible man and infallible composer.

Anyone tracing the life of Ferdinand Bauer soon realises how closely linked it is with that of his brother, Franz. Though he always remained on good terms with Johann and Josef, Franz was clearly Ferdinand's favourite brother. They were closest in age, shared the same art and science training, first under Pater Boccius in Feldsberg, later under Jacquin in Vienna, and both came under Sir Joseph Banks patronage while they were in London. Like Jacob and Wilhelm Grimm whose personal and scholarly partnership proved so fruitful for history, mythology and linguistics, the Bauer brothers, Franz and Ferdinand, enjoyed a very close working relationship which provided an extra dimension to their lives. They collaborated on a number of projects and worked together with the same botanists such as John Lindley. Even though Ferdinand spent five years in Australia while Franz remained at Kew, the latter was well aware of the places Ferdinand was visiting and the flora he was collecting. Indeed, he may well have helped to prepare him for the journey, since he had long been working with William Aiton on *Delineations of exotick plants cultivated in the Royal Garden at Kew (1796)* which featured Australian natives.

Both in London and Vienna, the Bauers shared the same circle of friends. They were accepted as equals by the scientists of the period and their scientific opinions as well as their magnificent illustrations were highly regarded. Their friends and acquaintances included many of the great names and they recur like a litany at the end of Ferdinand's letters to Franz from Australia. Among them were the geologist John Hawkins, William Aiton, Director of the Royal Botanical Gardens at Kew and Leopold Fitzinger, custodian of the K.K. Hofnaturaliencabinet in Vienna and, of course, Sir Joseph Banks and Robert Brown. Guy Meynell who has written an engrossing article on Franz Bauer[7] gives us an idea of his standing amongst English scientists when he quotes from a contemporary:

> [Bauer] recalled the best days of Sir Everard Home, who, we are told, for some length of time used to meet here, almost every Saturday, at Mr. Bauer's, many of the eminent men of the day, for purposes connected with Botany and other branches of Natural Philosophy and a friendly and social intercourse.[8]

Professionally, their paths diverged after Ferdinand's departure for Vienna when

Stylidium scandens

Franz became increasingly interested in anatomical and physiological drawings, and he began to collaborate with Sir Everard Home and with A.B. Granville on papers for the *Philosophical Transactions of the Royal Society*. He became one of the experts in microscopy (he was the proud owner of 16 different microscopes) and one of the earliest scientists concerned with photography. On February 8, 1821 Franz Bauer was elected to the Royal Society. Unlike Ferdinand he published several scientific papers. He was clearly more verbal than Ferdinand and his greater ease with English may have played a role in his ready assimilation into English society. This is indicated by his decision to change his name to Francis, his adoption of Anglicanism and his use of English rather than German in letters to his Austrian friend, Jacquin.

Ferdinand, on the other hand, clearly hated writing and as his letters show, was comfortable neither in English nor in German though he obviously preferred the latter. This may have played a part in his decision to return to Austria.

Neither Ferdinand nor Franz seem to have had any great ability in communicating their emotions. Only two letters reveal something of their feelings, the letter in which Ferdinand chides his brother for not writing and the letter which Franz wrote to Jan Lhotsky after reading the latter's biographical sketch on the anniversary of Ferdinand's death. Neither of them ever married and their closest friends seem to have been their scientific colleagues.

Franz and Ferdinand were equal in the mastery of their art and botanists often find it difficult to distinguish between their drawings though Franz did not use Ferdinand's elaborate colour code. While both succeeded in blending science and art in their work, Franz appears to have been the greater scientist and Ferdinand the more inspired artist.

The empathy and devotion of the two brothers was appreciated by their contemporaries and is best symbolised by the splendid memorial tablet erected to Franz Bauer inside St Anne's Church on Kew Green. It reads:

In Memoriam

Francis Bauer . . . In the delineation of plants he united the accuracy of a profound naturalist, with the skill of the accomplished artist, to a degree which has been only equalled by his brother Ferdinand. In microscopical drawing he was altogether unrivalled and science will be ever indebted for his elaborate illustrations of animals and vegetable structures . . . The *works* of Francis Bauer are his best *monument.* Friendship inscribes this record on his honoured tomb.

Ferdinand Bauer, like his brother, owed his outstanding artistic and scientific achievements to the talent inherited from his father and to a very supportive environment going hand in hand with excellent training. He was also fortunate that he was born into an age which was beginning to be very interested in the use of scientific instruments. His use of the microscope opened up possibilities unknown to earlier artists. With this was coupled Brown's interest in Jussieu's botanical system as against the strictly Linnaean system previously in vogue. This meant that Bauer perfected a method of presenting not only the reproductive parts of the plant but also the minutest detail of its seeds and pollen. Bauer, the artist, simultaneously had to meet the challenge of presenting the plant and its many botanical features as a unique artistic whole.

Ferdinand's personality displayed all the qualities that go to make a splendid craftsman — single-minded devotion, meticulousness, conscientiousness, unflagging energy. What set him apart from all his peers, was that one quality transcending the material aspects of the craft which is as unpredictable as it is inexplicable and which we call genius. Like Wolfgang Amadeus Mozart, Ferdinand Lucas Bauer was a child of the late baroque age, a period distinguished by a passion for form coupled with an exuberant spirit which delighted in playful embellishment. To understand Mozart, one must listen to his music; to gain insight into Bauer, one must look at his art. There are drawings of plants and of animals which, while remaining absolutely accurate representations of nature, reveal Ferdinand's compassion, humour and fantasy.

Perhaps it is no coincidence that Johann Wolfgang Goethe, who recognized the genius of Mozart, was also an admirer of Bauer's art. In his essay on flower painting, written in 1817, he devotes two pages to an analysis of Bauer's depiction of the pine tree in Lambert's *A Description of the Genus Pinus.* He had found Lambert's book in the Royal Library at Weimar and quotes Bauer's illustrations as the epitome of all that is best in botanical drawing and as a model to be followed by others. Goethe speaks of Bauer being 'one who is perfect in his art and knows how to turn it to his purposes in an original way' he goes on to say:

. . . daher wird man beim Anblick dieser Blätter bezaubert: die Natur ist offenbar, die Kunst versteckt, die Genauigkeit groß, die Ausführung mild, die Gegenwart entschieden und befriedigend.[9]

(. . . therefore we are enchanted at the sight of these leaves: nature is revealed, art concealed, great in its precision, gentle in its execution, decisive and satisfying in its appearance.)

After detailing all the elements that the botanical artist must consider in order to produce a satisfactory painting Goethe echoes Banks' comments when he says;

> That anyone might attempt to solve such a problem would not have occurred to us if we did not have before us a few pictures where the artist has achieved that which would strike all those merely trying to imagine it as completely impossible.

While Ferdinand the naturalist was acclaimed by his own age, Ferdinand the artist owes his rediscovery above all to William Stearn and Wilfrid Blunt who, in the 1950s, began to analyse his work from the perspective of art as well as science.[10] One can do no better than to quote Stearn's comments in the *Dictionary of Australian Artists* published as recently as 1984:

> For their elegance, their meticulous accuracy and their wealth of exquisite detail, Ferdinand Bauer's illustrations of Australian plants are the most beautiful and informative that have ever been made.[11]

Australia can consider itself fortunate that it had in Ferdinand Bauer an artist dedicated to the portrayal of its native flora and fauna. He was a genius, sensitive to Australia's unique beauty, with the knowledge, aesthetic sense and technical skill required to capture its true image for all time.

Notes

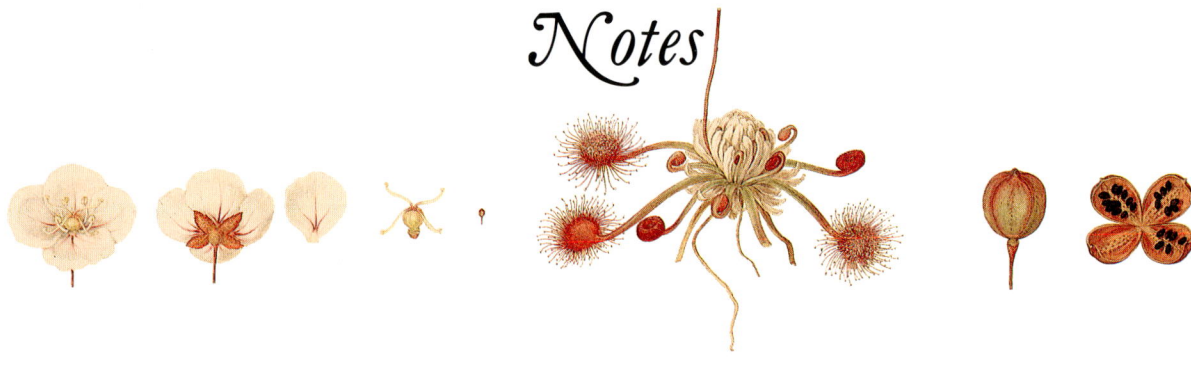

INTRODUCTION

1 Lhotsky, 1843, p.106
2 Lhotsky to Council of the Linnean Society, Archives of the Linnean Society

ARTISTIC APPRENTICESHIP

1 Lhotsky, 1843, p.106
2 Franz Bauer to Jan Lhotsky, Kew, 17.3.1839, Archives of the Linnean Society
3 Lhotsky, 1843, ibid.
4 *The Athenaeum*, 1840, no.687: 1025-1026
5 Lhotsky, 1843, p.107
6 Lhotsky, 1843, p.108
7 Maiden, 1909, p.71
8 Jacquin to Banks, Vienna, 17.4.1790, (unsigned), Vienna Autographs, University College London, MS ADD 254
9 Dolezal, H.: 'Zur Editionsgeschichte der *Icones Plantarum Rariorum* von Nicolaus Joseph von Jacquin in *Festschrift für Klaus Nissa Pressler*, Wiesbaden, 1973, p.151
10 Hooker, Joseph Dalton: *On the Flora of Australia*, London, 1859, p.cxiv

AUSTRALIAN ADVENTURE

1 Lhotsky, 1843, p.108
2 Ingleton, 1986, p.111
3 Matthew to Ann Flinders, 7.7.1801
4 Flinders, M: *Journal*, vol.1, Mitchell Library, MSS Safe 1/24
5 Good, 1981, p.42
6 ibid.
7 ibid.
8 Ferdinand to Franz Bauer, False Bay, 21.10.1801
9 Ferdinand to Franz Bauer, Simons Bay, 3.11.1801
10 Ferdinand to Franz Bauer, Sydney, 22.5.1802
11 Good, 1981, p.51
12 Flinders, *Journal*, vol.1, 9.1.1802
13 Good, 1981, p.54
14 Flinders, 1814, vol.1, p 110
15 Lhotsky, 1843, p.110
16 Ingleton, p.137
17 Ferdinand to Franz Bauer, Sydney, 22.5.1802
18 ibid.
19 Flinders, 1814, vol.1, p.148
20 ibid., p,170
21 ibid.
22 ibid., p.172
23 ibid., p.183
24 Ferdinand to Franz Bauer, Sydney, 22.5.1802
25 Good, 1981, p.75
26 Ferdinand to Franz Bauer, Sydney, 22.5.1802
27 Flinders to Banks, Sydney 20.5.1802
28 Brown to Banks, Sydney, 30.5.1802
29 Good, 1981, p.86
30 ibid., p.93
31 ibid., p.95
32 Ferdinand to Franz Bauer, at sea, 18.10.1802
33 Good, 1981, p.99
34 Flinders, 1814, vol.1, p.209
35 Ferdinand to Franz Bauer, Timor, 8.4.1803
36 Brown to Banks, Timor, March 1803
37 Flinders, 1814, vol.2, p.145
38 Ferdinand to Franz Bauer, Timor, 8.4.1803
39 Good, 1981, p.103
40 ibid.
41 ibid., p.104
42 ibid.
43 Stearn and Blunt, 1976
44 Good, 1981 p.105-6
45 ibid., p.106
46 ibid., p.107
47 ibid., p.108
48 ibid., p.109
49 ibid., p.114
50 ibid., p.115
51 Flinders, *Journal*, vol.1, 5.3.1803
52 Good, 1981, p.121
53 Ferdinand to Franz Bauer, Timor, 8.4.1803
54 ibid.
55 Good, 1981, p.122
56 *Historical Records of Australia*, series 1, vol.4, p.386

57 ibid., p.387
58 Brown to Banks, Sydney, 6.8.1803
59 Bauer to Banks, Sydney, 8.8.1803
60 Ferdinand to Joseph Bauer, Sydney, 8.8.1803
61 Lhotsky, 1843, p.109
62 *Historical Records of N.S.W.*, vol.5, p.509
63 Brown to Banks, Van Diemen's Land, 4.3.1804
64 Brown to Banks, Sydney, 12.12.1804
65 Ferdinand to Franz, Sydney, 7.3.1804
66 Bauer to Banks, at sea, 27.8.1804
67 *Historical Records of N.S.W.*, vol.5, p.387
68 Bauer to Banks, ibid.
69 Brown to Banks, Sydney, 12.12.1804
70 Endlicher, 1833, the English version is from an unpublished translation from the original Latin and was kindly made available to me by the author, Dr Alana Nobbs of Macquarie University, Sydney
71 Information from a manuscript by Mr Hicks, soon to be published
72 Austin, 1964
73 Brown to Banks, Sydney, 21.2.1805
74 King to Brown, Sydney, 22.7.1805
75 Mabberley, 1985, p.127
76 Brown to Marsden, London, 5.11.1805, British Museum, Add MSS 324 39f 186
77 Mabberley, 1985, p.128
78 Brown to Smith, London, 12.1.1806, in *Historical Records of N.S.W.*, vol.6, p.11
79 *Historical Records of N.S.W.*, vol.6, p.19
80 Banks to Marsden, London, January 1806, in *Historical Records of N.S.W.*, vol.6, p.17
81 Ingleton, 1986, p.379
82 Lhotsky, 1843, p.110
83 Wantrup, 1987, p.143
84 Lhotsky 1843, p.111
85 Franz Bauer to Joseph Jacquin, Kew, 20.9.1814, University College London, Vienna Autographs, Ms, Add, 254
86 Stafleu and Cowen, 1976
87 ibid.
88 Wantrup, 1987, p.147

RETURN TO AUSTRIA

1 Lhotsky, 1843, p.111
2 Lhotsky, 1843, p.112, Lhotsky is mistaken about these illustrations being miniatures, for details of Lindley and Lambert see bibliography
3 Bauer lists 19 animals, 158 birds, 36 amphibia, 28 fish and 18 insects for New Holland, making a total 259 zoological and 1283 botanical drawings. Norfolk Island yielded 39 zoological drawings (20 birds, 3 fish, 16 insects) and 21 botanical drawings

4 *Flora* 9, 1826, Bd.1. p.240, Königl. Bayr. Botanische Gesellschaft, Regensburg
5 Flora, 10, 1827, Bd. 1, p.76

THE INDEFATIGABLE MR BAUER

1 Lhotsky, 1843, p.112
2 Brown to Banks, Sydney, 30.5.1802 and 6.8.1803; Banks to Brown, London, 9.4.1803
3 Ingleton, 1986, p.435
4 Matthew to Ann Flinders, Sydney, 25.6.1803, (draft) in Flinders, *Private Letter Book*, vol.1, Mitchell Library, MSS Safe 1/54
5 Blunt, 1950, p.9
6 Hill, 1941
7 Meynell, 1983, p.209-221
8 Sheer, F.: *Kew and its gardens*, Steill, London, 1841, p.36n
9 Goethe, J.W.: 'Blumenmalerei' in *Kunstschriften*, Band II, Insel, Leipzig, 1912 (Großherzog Wilhelm Ernst Ausgabe), p.423/24
10 Blunt, 1950
11 Stearn, W.; in *Dictionary of Australian Artists*, Kerr J. (Ed.), Power Institute of Fine Arts, Sydney, 1984 p.58

Appendix

Ten letters which Ferdinand wrote from Australia have come to light. Eight of these were written in German, seven were addressed to Franz Bauer at Kew and one to his brother Josef in Vienna. These letters are held by the Linnean Society in London having been presented to the Society by Jan Lhotsky. The two letters in English are addressed to Sir Joseph Banks in London: the first is held by the British Museum and the second by the Royal Botanic Gardens at Kew.

The Language of Ferdinand Bauer's Letters

Ferdinand Bauer's letters are, as we have seen, not a particularly rich source of his activities or his feelings. They do, however, throw an interesting light on his spoken language. Born before tape recorders, Bauer has left us no auditory record but his phonetic spelling and his original syntax provide excellent clues for anyone wishing to reconstruct his speech. We know from contemporaries that Franz, though he lived in England for 50 years, always retained a strong German accent; Ferdinand's letters provide the strongest evidence that this accent reflected Austrian German.

Translating Ferdinand's German letters for the first time posed serious problems, since it was impossible to give a fair account, in translation, of writing that verges on the illiterate. It could all too easily lead to a quite mistaken belief that Ferdinand was either stupid or uneducated. What the letters in fact indicate is that the pen unlike the pencil and the brush was not his instrument. He obviously did not enjoy writing and used every possible excuse to avoid it. His German spelling and grammar are ever more erratic than was usual at the time and suggest that he did not have a firm grasp of the written language before switching to English at the age of 26, when he began to work for Sibthorp. Occasionally, one feels that he may even have suffered from dyslexia, a condition which is apparently not uncommon amongst those who are very strongly visually oriented.

Ferdinand's English letters suggest that he had no formal instruction in the language but simply picked it up by ear. While this must have made life very difficult for him and probably added to his uncertainties in German, it makes his letters a sensitive sound recording of his own speech and of the English accents that he heard around him.

The German letters are written in the old German script except when Ferdinand quotes English names or expressions (e.g. partnership) and, as was the custom, switches to Roman script.

Those engaged in teaching English as a second language will feel on very familiar ground with Ferdinand's letters to Sir Joseph, but for those not fortunate enough to have chosen this rewarding profession a short 'Bauer dictionary' may be helpful:

bleased— pleased
pranch— branch
poat— boat
Karbontaria— Carpentaria
Passes Street— Bass Strait
Moden Bird Island— Mutton Bird Island

Like most Austrians, Ferdinand does not distinguish between the sounds 'b' and 'p'; 'd' and 't'; 'g' and 'k'. He has the same uncertainty in German where he tries every variation of 'gedenken' (to think of) from 'gedängen' to 'getängen' and 'getänken'.

Here are some more examples:

emploiad— employed
aprensive— apprehensive
oppertunity— opportunity
Blew Mountings— Blue Mountains
con— come
I have prosid— I have proceeded
be acquaint— been acquainted
Poart Jacsen— Port Jackson
pense— pains
couse— course

Ferdinand does not spell according to the rules. In some cases he spells as he speaks ('poart' and 'pens'); in others as he hears those around him speak, adding sounds ('mountings') or swallowing them ('aprensive').

Some of his strange uses are direct translations from German. Thus 'by every opportunity' (instead of 'at') is taken from the German 'bei jeder Gelegenheit'. On the other hand, his German has been influenced by English. For example 'I foresee' is translated into German as 'ich vorsehe' and 'für mich' becomes 'vor mich' by analogy with 'for me'.

The idiosyncratic punctuation is obviously an indication of his phrasing but in the English translations punctuation has been standardized in the interest of easier reading. In order to show Bauer's style, I have followed the original as closely as possible, but have not reproduced his errors in the translation.

*Letter to his brother Franz at Kew Gardens received
23 January 1802*

*False Bay on board the
Investigator. Oct 21st 1801*

Dear Brother,

I am taking the first opportunity to send you a letter from here to let you know that the Investigator arrived safely in False Bay off the Cape of Good Hope. We had a journey of almost 3 months since our departure from England, 4 days of which we spent calling in on the island of Madeira, and I would have written to you from there if I had not heard that the ship was going to remain there for some time whereupon we went into the mountains for a few days. Upon our return we found the ship ready to sail so that I had neither the time to write to you nor the opportunity to send a letter, and I hope that this finds you well and in good health. As far as I am concerned I must admit that I have enjoyed very good health to date except for some days when I was plagued by a sore throat and headache and, to my great surprise, I found that from the time I first set foot on the ship till this moment I have not felt the slightest touch of any sea sickness.

I have hopes that we will stay here for some time because the ship requires extensive repairs and I am sorry to say that throughout the entire voyage so far we seldom had a dry cabin because water was coming in everywhere through the sides of the upper-middle deck despite the fact that during this time we were not exposed to any great storm. From here our journey is to take us directly to King Georges Sound in New Holland for which we will, presumably, head from here within 3 weeks.

Now to tell you a little about the Cape of Good Hope. The bay in which we landed is large and surrounded by mountains at the foot of which is situated a small town which consists of only a few houses in which little or nothing is to be had. The mountains, however, which are for the most part large sand hills are covered with the most beautiful plants so that our first excursion yielded us a great number of the most beautiful blooms, of these I wish I could send to you in England all the orchid types which I have seen so far. I have already collected various drawings of everything and this is the place and a great opportunity for collecting. We are thinking of going on a journey to Capetown and Table Mountain and when I return I shall write to you again. In the meantime I would ask you to remember me to all our friends in London and to excuse me for not writing to many of them. Remember me above all to Sir J. Banks, Mr Walker, Mr Hawkins, Mr Lambert and to Gruber, Eichner, Fitzinger and I wish you may, in the meantime, continue in good health and spirits and remain your

*sincere brother
Ferd Bauer*

Appendix

Simons Bay
3 Nov 1801

Dear Brother,

I hope you received my letter of the 18th October from False Bay which I sent off on the second day after our arrival and today, the 3rd of November, it has been decided to depart for King Georges Sound, New Holland. I must admit, however, that I am not happy to be leaving this area so soon because of the great number of beautiful things which could be found here if one had more time to look for them. Our journey on foot over Table Mountain to Capetown was rather arduous but I am glad I undertook it because we saw much that was beautiful in the way of botany above all the Orchites Proteax and much else which I do not have the time to enumerate and will, (indeed), have to close before doing so, although I can foresee that we will not be able to hear from one another for a long time. I embrace you and hope that you may remain throughout this time in constant health and good spirits. It is to be presumed that we will reach Port Jackson in April of next year and will, in the meantime, have visited the coasts from King Georges Sound to Port Jackson. Should you wish to write to me during this time or should you have some letters for me, send them at the first opportunity, also send some newspapers containing the most interesting things which have happened in Europe during this time, and address them to

> Col: Paterson for Mr. Bauer on board His Majesties Ship Investigator, Port Jackson, New South Wales

I would like you to remember me to all my friends in London and to give my regards to Sir J. Banks, Mr. Greville, Mr. Walker etc. etc.

Fare you well,
I remain your sincere brother
Ferd Bauer

If you get into town go and see Mr. Obüt and let him know that I have written to my agents Messers W & Chas Prater No. 6 Charing Cross asking them to withdraw my salary and pay his bill with it as soon as they can get the money.

May 22nd 1802 Sydney Cove on
Board
the Investigator

Dear Brother,

I hope that you received both my letters from the Cape of Good Hope. This is my first opportunity since then to send you a letter from which you can see that we arrived safely in Sydney Cove on the 9th of May. After a journey of 5 weeks from the Cape we got to see the land of New Holland for the first time on 7 December 1801 after which, on the 8th, we anchored in King Georges Sound and remained there till the 4 January 1802 in the course of which we made a number of short land excursions during which we found many new plants. From King Georges Sound which we left on the 4th of January we sailed east along the as yet quite unknown coast of New Holland, where in several places we found a great number of islands some of which are quite large and there were also found along the coast a number of rivers or entries from the sea and large bays in which we frequently dropped anchor. This coast kept us busy till the middle of April when we came into Bass Strait and from there, on the 9th of May, into Port Jackson. On the southwest coast we met the French ship, the Geographe, with Capt. Baudin which was travelling on an English passport for the same purpose as the Investigator. The land which we saw on this coast looks very barren for the most part and consists largely of sand hills which are partly covered with shrubs while others are quite bare. Further inland, however, it is heavily timbered and in many places the trees have been burned down. We found very few inhabitants on this land and none at all on the islands if we are not going to count the kangaroos as such, of which we found very many on the islands. Although the season for plants in bloom had almost passed in New Holland, I nevertheless made 350 sketches of plants besides 100 sketches of the animal kingdom during this time. We would have considered ourselves fortunate to have completed this part of the journey which in several places, especially between the islands, is very dangerous, if we had not had the misfortune to lose the master of our ship, Mr. Thistle, a midshipman, Mr. Taylor, and 6 sailors in a boat which went to the shore and from there back to the ship. Otherwise, most were in good health during this time. As far as I am concerned, although we were exposed to great heat and great fatigue in the course of our land excursions, I am nevertheless in good health and spirits and I wish that my letter may find you the same though I scarcely expect to hear this for another 12 months which will be the time when we are expected to put in here again.

In the meantime, I would ask you to convey my respects to all my friends and acquaintances in London and Kew and to excuse me for not writing to all of them. Here, also, I have a lot of work but I will write to you again before we leave here and to Sir J. Banks too, to whom you should give my particular regards. You may receive your letter before he does. Also give my regards to Mr. Walker, Mr. Lambert, Mr. Hawkins and Gruber, Fitzinger etc. etc. etc. and I hope that you may, in the meantime, remain in good health and spirits.

I remain your sincere brother
Ferdinand Bauer

Letter to his brother Franz
{found together with a copy in another hand which shows slight variations}

---

on Board His Mjsty Ship
Investigator
Sydney Cove New South Wales
July 20th 1802

Dear Brother,

The two letters I sent you from the Cape of Good Hope and the one after our arrival in Sydney Cove on the 10th of May have, I hope, reached you and this one will acquaint you with the fact that the Investigator was ready on the morning of the 21st July to sail from Port Jackson bound for the east coast of New Holland and the Gulf of Carpentaria in the *north. I hope we will complete this cruise together with our companion, Lady Nelson, safely and in good health. I expect to write to you about this journey in approximately 10 to 12 months time.*

I was full of great expectations that I would receive a letter from you while we were in Sydney but though 6 ships arrived here from England none brought a letter for me.

I have so far always found much to occupy me. We made several short excursions inland, for example to Botany Bay, Parramatta and Hawkesbury and from there to the river Grose which brought us to the foot of the Blue Mountains after which I returned to Sydney with the Lady Nelson on the Hawkesbury River. During this time I made considerable additions to my collection and all my sketches which now number 700 I have left behind in the Governor's house [for safe keeping?].

Forgive me for not writing in greater detail but that we will have to leave for the future, in the meantime I wish you health and good cheer and I ask that you remember me again to all my friends in London.

> *Fare you well*
> *I remain your sincere brother*
> *Ferd Bauer*

Letter to his brother Franz in Kew Gardens received 10 October 1803

> *His Majsty Ship Investigator at sea*
> *October 18, 1802*

Dear Brother,

I am taking this opportunity just to let you know that the Investigator has come along this coast as far as the Cumberland Islands and between the Coral Reefs, where this night we lay at anchor and where I heard that the brig Lady Nelson was going back to Port Jackson. About myself I can only report that I am very well as are all on our ship and that so far there has been no particular accident except to the boat and the anchor although the coast on this side is extremely dangerous. I have made good additions to our collection during this time.

> *Fare you well*
> *your sincere brother*
> *Ferdinand Bauer*

[In the left margin]: Give my respects to all my friends in London and in Vienna when you write.

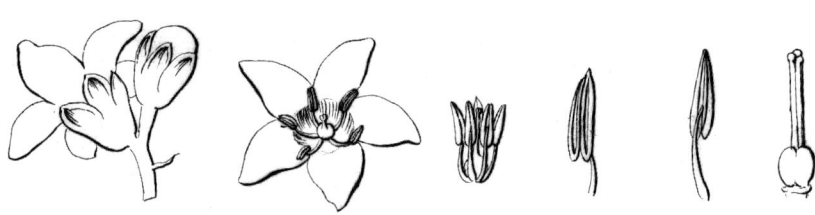

Letter to his brother Franz at Kew Gardens received May 12, 1804

Timor, April 8 1803

Dear Brother,

I am glad to have the opportunity of writing to you again to tell you a little about what has been happening to us since my last letter, which I hope you received before this one and which was written in the Coral Reefs on the 18th of October 1802 when the brig Lady Nelson left us to return to Port Jackson and the Investigator went on her way to Endeavour Strait. We had a favourable wind which soon brought us to the Strait, sailed through Torres Strait, passed by the Murray Islands and then came to the Prince of Wales Island from which we arrived in the Gulf of Carpentaria on the 3rd of November. We had high expectations of the Gulf of Carpentaria but found that the whole of the side facing east is very low-lying country with very shallow water for a long distance so that our ship could not come close. We only came ashore once at Coen River and that only for a short period. At the end of the Gulf towards the Strait you can, for the most part, only see the land from the mast of the ship. Turning to the west we came upon many islands. The coast also begins to rise more steeply and the water to become deeper. Amongst the islands we put down anchor several times in order to load water. We also landed on the shore of the Gulf, chiefly in Arnhem's Land, which gave us the opportunity to visit the surrounding area about which we will talk more at a later time. It seems that after Captain Flinders' survey, the Gulf of Carpentaria will remain as it appeared in the old charts with a few changes.

On our way past the Murray Islands we had a strong wind which caused a lot of water to enter the ship which was then examined when we lay at anchor in the Gulf. It was found that the main part of the timbers and the side walls were completely rotten and mouldy and that the ship could not be guaranteed to last for six months on the high sea whereupon Cap. Flinders was of a mind to head straight for Port Jackson as soon as he had finished in the Gulf. At the end of February 1803 we left the Gulf and on the 6th of March we departed from the north coast of New Holland and put out to sea. We had, however, very little and an unfavourable wind for 3 weeks which brought us into the area around Timor. During this time the ship was again examined but it was found that the decay of the ship's timber had not increased much since the last examination, whereupon Cap. Flinders decided to go to Timor thinking that if the ship could be repaired a little it could certainly last longer on the sea and if he could get provisions in Timor for another cruise, he would like to finish the north and west coast of New Holland before going to Port Jackson. We will know this with more certainty when we reach Timor.

As far as I am concerned I can tell you that I have, during all this time, been in good health and spirits although one does suffer a good deal from the heat in this latitude. The ship's company was also fortunate in this regard and had few sick men but now, just recently, many show evidence of scurvy.

With regard to Natural History I have, since we left Port Jackson, made sketches of 500 species of plants but only 90 of animals, mostly birds. I have not completed anything and will not be able to do so either. The paper which I took with me on this cruise has gone mouldy because of the dampness and warmth of the cabin and is covered with spots of mould and can no longer be painted on or used for any kind of painting.

I am very much looking forward to finding letters from you and hearing some news when we reach Sydney. I hope that you have been in good health and spirits till now and will

Banksia pulchella

continue so during the time of my absence until we have the pleasure of seeing each other again. I embrace you and once again wish you good health and spirits.

> *I remain your sincere brother*
> *Ferdinand Bauer*

I have to trouble you with another commission, through which you would, however, do me a great favour and that is that you give Sir Joseph Banks my regards and tell him what you have heard of me and what I have been doing on this expedition. I would have written to Sir J. B. but now I think I will leave it till we reach Port Jackson and I can see what is going to happen to the expedition once the ship Investigator has been condemned.

[On the envelope]: *Give my regards to all my friends and acquaintances in London and when you are with Dr. Grun give my apologies for not writing to him but it is really too warm to write many letters here.*

Dear Brother

Cap. Flinders has decided to go directly from Timor to Port Jackson and tomorrow, April 8, the Investigator will sail from here. We have received great courtesy from the Governor of Timor who is a German.

> *Fare you well*

Letter to his brother Franz at Kew Gardens received 26 July 1804

> *Farm Cove Sydney March 7 1804*

Dearest Brother,

I have not missed any opportunity of writing to you when I was able to send you a letter and hope that my last ones as also this one will find you in good health and spirits and with great yearning I long to hear this from you. A long time has passed and there must have been opportunities to write to me but I have not received one letter from you.

Capt. Flinders has I hope by this time arrived safely in England. He sailed from Sydney on the 20 September on the Cumberland Sloop. Through him and through my letters which he brought you, you will have learnt how he and we fared on our previous journey; now I have come to the point of wishing very much that he would soon come out with another ship and end this voyage. You will presumably be able to hear at Sir Joseph Banks' house what is being said and thought about the Investigator's voyage, also what is to happen in the future; as soon as you hear something and know what is going on, you would to me a great favour if you would write and tell me at the first opportunity.

As far as I am concerned, I can tell you that I have kept good health since our transportation and have increased my collection by several hundred during this time. But now the plants are beginning to be rarer and one has to go further to find something new and anyway I think New Holland is not as rich in plants as I thought. I also went several times some distance inland and to the Blue Mountains as far as my feet would let me but did not manage to go a great distance. As far as I can see and hear no one has got very far. After our arrival in Sydney when we left the ship, Mr. Brown and I rented a house and lived together but our partnership did not last long, whereupon I took a house in Farm Cove a mile from Sydney where I live alone and undisturbed. Mr. Brown left for Van Diemen's Land and has already gone.

Facsimile of a page of Ferdinand's letter to Franz, 7 March 1804 (see p. 106 for translation).
By permission of the Council of the Linnean Society of London.

Give my respects to Sir J. Banks I wanted to write to him but have no more to say than I reported in my last letter. {indecipherable} I cannot send anything because I have as yet nothing finished: My idea is to make sketches of everything that I get which can then be completed when the opportunity occurs. Here I cannot know what will then be {indecipherable} good use of my time.

Give my regards to all my friends especially Mr. J. Walker, Mr. Hawkins, Mr. Lambert, Mr. Aiton and do not forget Dr. Gruber, Mr. Fitzinger and Fischer. It only remains to wish you good health and good spirits and I remain your sincere

Brother Ferd Bauer

[On envelope] *In the letters which Capt. Flinders brought you I asked you to send me half a ream of cartridge and half a ream of large brown wrapping paper when he came out again to conclude our voyage. I beg you not to forget it.*

[Note by Franz on the envelope]: *Ferdinand in 1805 still in Norfolk Island and I expect that because of Capt. Flinders' fate their return will take place in 1807.*

Letter to his brother Joseph in Vienna

Sydney, New South Wales
August 8th, 1803

Dear Brother,

We are now far away from each other and perhaps that makes one think more about each other than when one is close and has more opportunity to hear from each other. Since you received my last letter I have been in Australia or New Holland which we have almost circumnavigated twice, and now the time of our absence is going to be much increased because of the ship which was found, after its second circling of this island or continent, to be unfit to leave port for a further journey. Whereupon the Commander decided to go to England and bring out another ship in order to save the voyage: we, the naturalist and I, have decided to stay in Sydney, an English colony in New Holland, and wait for the return of the Captain or till we get news from the Government which will take at least 10 or 12 months.

I have during this time collected much Natural History in Australia and other distant parts and can report that I have, despite the fact that one has to suffer considerable discomfort in these parts because of the great heat, enjoyed good health throughout the entire voyage and I would be glad to know the same of you. In the meantime, I wish that it may be so with all my heart and that you may continue in good spirits. Adieu I

remain your
devoted
Brother Ferd Bauer

Be sure to give my regards to all our friends and relations in and around Vienna.

Appendix

Letter to Sir Joseph Banks in Soho Square, London

Sydney, August 8, 1803

Sir,

I am sorry and beg you will excuse that I have so long omitted to give you an account of my proceeding in the time of the Investigator Voyage to which you have been bleased {sic} to recommend me.

In any opinnion I resolved that in such an expedition it will be the best by every opportunitis to preserve as many subjects of Natural history in sketches as shall be in my power to execute; for fear to loss some which might be new or rare before they are asertained; in this manner I have prosid & now have collected from New Holland in sketches of plants above one Thousand and of Animals two Hunderd {sic}, from this can be select the new or best which may be at any time finished & I am sorry that I have not any finished Drawings to send by this opportunity for in the time of the voyage I was most occupied with the sketches until a little befor our arreival {sic} in Port Jackson & after Capt Flinders determination of going to England, things have been unsettled that little mor could have been don.

This unexpected determination of Cap Flinders; requierd much consideration, to take such part which maight be to your departments advantageous, if an object of the Voyage we have undertaken & if such should be finished: our stay in New South Wales would add much to the collections and if not new subjects could be procurt I would be able to finish some from them wath I have already made, and must bej done in England.

therefor our stay in New South Wales would be mor to the interest for our engagemend & has occasiond my resollution to remain here, in expectation I hope it will be approved of.

> *I have the honous*
> *to be*
> *Sir*
> *Your Most Obd*
> *Humble & faithfull*
> *Servant*
> *Ferdinand Bauer*

Ferdinand Bauer

Letter to Sir Joseph Banks in Soho Square, London

at Sea in the way to
Norfolk Island
Augst 27th 1804

I shall not omit by this opportunity to acquaint you how I have emploiad the time in New South Wales since the departure of Capt Flinders who I hope has had the good fortune to arrive safe in England, from him and our letters send by him You will have acquaint of the couse of our Stay in this Country.

Soon after the sailing of Capt Flinders from Port Jackson Mr Brown also left this place and went to the South of Van Diemens land, and is not yet returnd from the Derwent, which has left me for this part of the Country to myself, and I am verry glad that I remain here in this fine spring season in which many plants have been in flower which not have been seen before, and I have found in places wher I have been many times befor this two years after another we have been the same season at Port Jackson. I also made in this time various excursions in to the Country, so far as the Blue Mountings and the Cowpasturs to Mount Hunter, and the Riveres; Grose, Nepean, Hokesbury, Georges River and to Newcastle the new settlement at the Coal or Hunters River, all this places have add and much enlarged our collections.

I am sorry to sae that I have not anything finished to send home by this oppertunity, all that I have collect and don consist in sketches and matherials from which Drawings or Engravings at any time can be made, from such which will be New or rare, I am aprensive I would spend the time to finish some which might have been publishedd since we left England, and I would loss many which might be New, has ocasiont that I have made a collection of sketches of allmost all the plants of New Holland which did con {come} to my hands & I flatter myself when the Investigator Vojage should come to a happy conclution the pense which I have taken to give satisfaction in that pranch of science which was alotted to me will met with approvation, with which I remain in hope

& am Sir
Your
Most Humble Most Obedient
Servant
Ferd Bauer

Having heard that the produce of Norfolk Island are so different from this of New Holland, I tuk the opportunity to go with Capt. Bunker of the Ship Albion, the convoyer of this letter who in his passage to England will leave me there, which will give me a time of two month to stay at the Island, when the Investigators Ship will be finished, and come to remove the settlers with whom I shall return to Port Jackson.

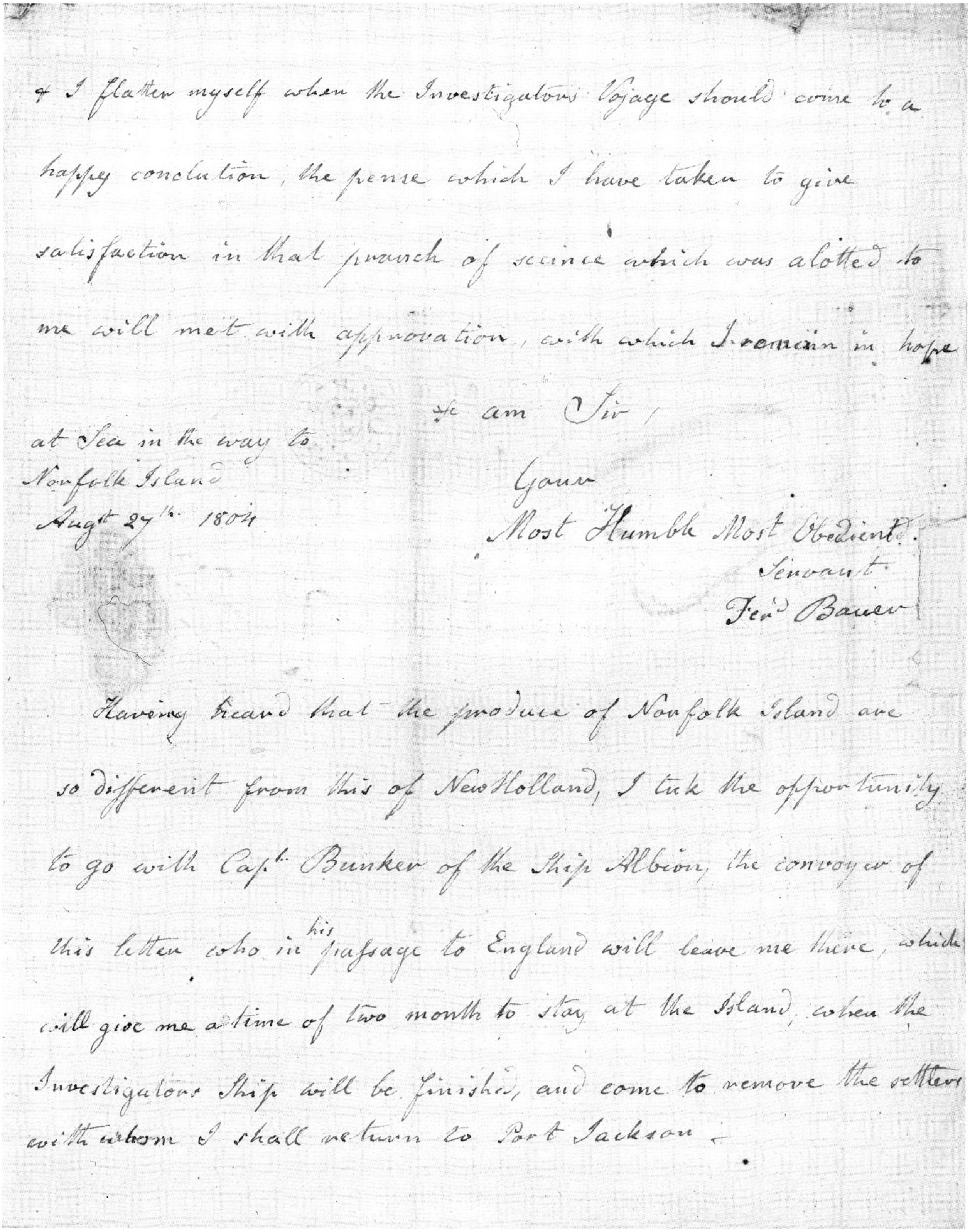

& I flatter myself when the Investigator's Voyage should come to a

happy conclution, the pense which I have taken to give

satisfaction in that pranch of science which was alotted to

me will met with approvation, with which I remain in hope

&c am Sir,

at Sea in the way to
Norfolk Island

Aug.st 27.th 1804

Your

Most Humble Most Obedient

Servant

Ferd Bauer

    Having heard that the produce of Norfolk Island are

so different from this of New Holland, I tuk the opportunity

to go with Cap.t Bunker of the Ship Albion, the convoyer of

this letter who in his passage to England will leave me there, which

will give me a time of two month to stay at the Island, when the

Investigators Ship will be finished, and come to remove the settlers

with whom I shall return to Port Jackson.

Facsimile of the last page of Bauer's letter to Sir Joseph Banks, 27 August 1804 (see p. 110).

TRANSLATION OF AN EXTRACT OF BAUER'S LAST WILL AND TESTAMENT

Secondly: I appoint as my universal heirs my three natural brothers of whom Johann Bauer is presently in Feldsberg, Josef Bauer in Vienna and Franz Bauer in England. These have, henceforth, to divide between themselves my invested capital as well as my savings and money in cash. Similarly they are equal heirs to my dwelling in Schmidgasse No. 155 in Hietzing in such a manner that if one of them wishes to take possession of the house, he is to be allowed to do so on payment of the valuer's price. Similarly my herbaria, birds, insects, shells and the drawings which belong to them are to be valued. Should one of my brothers wish to pay the valuer's price he shall be obliged to pay the other two parts. Should this not be the case the effects should be auctioned.

Thirdly: My library together with all that belongs to it I leave to my friend, Mr. Heinrich Schott, Imperial and Royal Chief Gardener, Adjutant, also my microscope.

Fourthly: My completed drawings of Greece and Australia I leave solely to my brother, Franz, presently resident in England.

Fifthly: The following are to be auctioned—a book with fifteen copperplate illustrations of the flora of Nova Hollandia as also the remaining drawings; my clothing, linen, bedding, furnishings and the profit shall be given to the universal heirs.

Facsimile of part of Bauer's last will and testament (Archives, Vienna Town Hall)

The Vienna Drawings

CHRISTA RIEDL-DORN

The Department of Botany at the Vienna Natural History Museum is in possession of a collection of more than 2000 drawings by Ferdinand Bauer, including a few watercolour paintings. The main bulk comprises pencil sketches made by Bauer during his five years in Australia and includes drawings from Norfolk Island, the Cape of Good Hope and the Island of Timor. There are a number of drawings of alpine plants, from an earlier period in Bauer's career as a botanical illustrator, made for the Prince of Liechtenstein and a few plates, showing different flowers arranged in a highly artistic way, which were obviously purely ornamental. They were all obtained by the Emperor, Franz I, at an auction soon after Bauer's death in 1826. The collection was transferred by order of the Emperor to the 'Botanisches Hofcabinet', predecessor of the present Department of Botany, Vienna Natural History Museum. In his report to the Court for 1826, Leopold Trattinick, Curator of Botany since the foundation of the 'Hofcabinet' in 1807, wrote:

> The botanical heritage of Ferdinand Bauer, who died in Hietzing in March of this year, consisting of 113 small parcels of dried plants fron New Holland, the Island of Timor, the Island of Norfolk and the Cape of Good Hope, and of 1876 plates of drawings of the same (sketched in pencil), which his Highest Imperial Majesty had purchased, has been handed over to me. At the K.K. Museum on the last of October 1826
>
> Leopold Trattinick, Curator

These drawings, as well as the herbarium sheets mentioned by Trattinick, were among those objects in Bauer's last will that were left to his brothers after his death (see p. 112). He had brought them with him to Vienna when he left England in 1814, while the finished illustrations of plants he had seen and drawn on the Flinders expedition had remained in London and are now preserved at the British Museum (Natural History). In his will Bauer had proposed that they should be sold at a public auction, which seems to have taken place very soon after he died. A list was prepared of the drawings according to the numbers Bauer had given them himself as well as according to their systematic position. Names were mentioned for all those specimens that had already been identified, while for the rest the numbers were considered sufficient for the moment.

From the notes in Trattinick's reports we know that Diesing, a zoologist, had borrowed a considerable number of drawings soon after they came to the 'Hofcabinet', though his purpose is not at all clear. Diesing had published papers on botanical subjects, but these were exclusively on algae. He had been a contemporary of Stephan Ladislaus Endlicher, one of the foremost botanists of his time, who followed Trattinick as curator of the botanical collections, and who later became the director of the Botanical Garden and Institute of Vienna University, following the younger Jacquin (Joseph Franz). During this time, the collections and library of the 'Botanisches Hofcabinet' were transferred to the University Institute, as Endlicher wanted to have everything together in one place. In 1875 the botanical collections, as well as that part of the library which was already at the University Institute before the amalgamation, were removed again and found their final home at the newly built K.K. Hofsmuseum. Diesing seems to have kept Bauer's drawings for a considerable time, but they had certainly been returned before his death.

Another episode in the history of the drawings relates to a letter written by the famous British botanist George Bentham to Endlicher. Dated 'London, 10 March, 1834' Bentham thanks Endlicher warmly for his offer to send him plates of Australian plants by Bauer, and states that he could not refuse such a 'magnanimous' offer. There is no doubt that Bentham had seen several of Bauer's drawings when he prepared his flora of Australia, especially members of the family Labiatae, for which he was the foremost authority in his time. Identifications in his handwriting have been found on some of the drawings. Nevertheless, he seems to have returned everything he got from Vienna.

A small collection of Bauer's drawings that turned up at Kew quite recently does not seem to have any connection with the Bentham loan, although Bentham did visit Vienna in the early 1830s. The drawings, which bear two numbers in Bauer's handwriting (one of them the collection number given to them by him), were among those purchased by the Emperor and kept in Vienna and were mentioned by Günther Beck von Managetta in a list prepared in 1883. Beck made a great inventory of all the holdings of the Department of Botany, when he took over the curatorship after Reichardt's untimely death on 2 August 1885, and only included what he had actually seen. We do not know how and when they came to England.

There is, however, another peculiarity in Beck's list that should be mentioned. While Trattinick gave the total number of 'Australian' drawings as 1876, in Beck's list 1970 sheets are enumerated. During Trattinick's time, 55 drawings had been listed as missing from Bauer's original numbers. It is interesting to speculate what happened during almost fifty years to produce an additional 94 drawings. A possible explanation could be that a number of drawings in indian ink, prepared by

some other person from Bauer's originals, had been added at a later date. There is, however, no conclusive evidence of this, but a fact in favour of this explanation is in Trattinick's report, where he only mentions the pencil drawings he received from the Emperor.

A recent discovery could help to shed some light on the question of the 55 drawings that were missing from the beginning. There are a small number of orginal drawings by Bauer from Australia included in the collection of botanical illustrations of Heinrich Wilhelm Schott, director of the Imperial Gardens at Schönbrunn, who died in 1865 and left all his personal belongings to his son Eugen. Eugen Schott agreed to hand over his father's books, 1379 herbarium sheets of Araceae, for which he had been a well-known authority, and the drawings still in his possession to the Natural History Museum in 1882 after some hesitation and bargaining. H.W. Schott had been mentioned in Bauer's last will: he was to receive his scientific library (see p. 112). Obviously, they had been on good terms during the last years of Bauer's life, when Schott had purchased a small house in Hietzing, then a suburb of Vienna and quite close to Schönbrunn Gardens, where Bauer seems to have been a regular visitor and to have drawn and painted plants cultivated there.

In 1889 Beck von Managetta ordered all the illustrations, which had hitherto been kept separate, to be inserted into the herbarium with the respective dried plant specimens. This decision proved fatal to a great number of valuable illustrations. In the case of Bauer, not all the drawings had actually been transferred to the herbarium, a few hundred were kept in the library. Whenever a loan of plant specimens belonging to a particular group was requested by some other institution, the drawings were sent along with them. A fire in 1945, at one of the depositories to which the collections had been removed for security reasons during World War II, destroyed a great number of pictures along with the dried plants. At the moment we can only guess as to how many of Bauer's drawings were lost in this way. Among the plant groups destroyed were all kinds of lillies, sedges, the famous Australian grass trees, beeches, oaks, birches, willows and poplars and related species, magnolias, the cock's foot family and many others.

During the last two decades, all the illustrations have been removed from the herbarium whenever staff members have come across them. However, it is difficult to proceed systematically in sorting them out because their treatment as herbarium specimens has led to frequent changes in the names originally applied to them as a consequence of revisions and new taxonomic concepts. Thus the old lists still in existence are of little help in finding them. Moreover, plants that had not been identified in the lists may have been put under the name that seemed most appropriate to someone engaged in inserting them into the herbarium without noting this in the lists or even without labelling them. From recent findings it is fairly likely that such a procedure has actually occurred. It will take some time before all the drawings left are united again in the collection of botanical art and illustration in the recently founded archive of the Department of Botany.

In spite of all these obstacles it will be one of the main tasks in the Department of Botany during the next few years to collect together all of Bauer's drawings to make them accessible to a wider public and to gain for him the fame as an artist and keen observer of plants that he deserves.

Bibliography

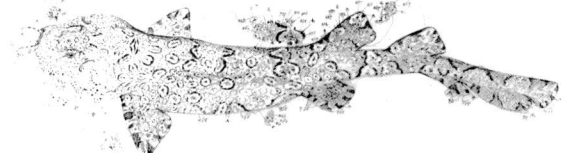

AUSTIN, K.A.: *The Voyage of the Investigator 1801-1803 — Commander Matthew Flinders — R.N.*, Rigby, Adelaide, 1964.

BLUNT, W.: *The Art of Botanical Illustration*, Collins, London, 1950.

BRITTEN, J.: 'Ferdinand Bauer's Drawings of Australian Plants' in *Journal of Botany*, vol.47, London, April 1909.

BURBIDGE, N.T.: 'Robert Brown's Collecting Localities' in *Proc. Linn. Soc.*, New South Wales. no.80, 1956.

DESMOND, R.: *Dictionary of British and Irish Botanists and Horticulturalists Including Plant Collectors and Botanical Artists*, Taylor and Francis, London, 1977.

EDWARDS, P. (Ed.): 'The Journal of Peter Good — Gardener on Matthew Flinders Voyage to Terra Australis, 1801-03, *Bulletin British Museum (Natural History) Historical Series, vol.9. London, 1981.*

EDWARDS, P.: 'Botany of Flinders' Voyage' in *People and Plants in Australia*, Carr, D.J. & S.J. (Eds.), Academic Press, Sydney, 1981.

FLINDERS, M.: *A Voyage to Terra Australis*, two volumes and atlas, Nicol, London, 1814.

FLINDERS, M.; *Reise nach dem Austral-Lande*, translated from the English by Götze, F., Verlag des Landes-Industrie-Comptoirs, Weimar, 1816.

HILL, E: *My Love Must Wait — The Story of Matthew Flinders*, Angus and Robertson. Sydney, 1941.

Historical Records of Australia, series 1, vol.4, 1803–June 1804, Library Committee of the Commonwealth Parliament, 1915.

Historical Records of N.S.W., vol.4-6, Government Printer, Sydney, 1896ff.

INGLETON, G.C.: *Matthew Flinders — Navigator and Chartmaker*, Genesis, Surrey, 1986.

LACK, E.: *Die Abenteuer des Sir Joseph Banks 1743-1820 — Botaniker, Weltreisender und Mäzen*, Böhlau, Vienna, 1985.

LHOTSKY, J.: 'Biographical Sketch of Ferdinand Bauer' in *Proceedings of the Linnean Society*, vol.1, London, 1839.

LHOTSKY, J.: 'Biographical Sketch of Ferdinand Bauer, Natural History Painter to the Expedition of Captain Flinders, R.N., to Terra Australis' in *London Journal of Botany*, Hooker (Ed.), vol.2, 1843.

MABBERLEY, D.J.: *Jupiter Botanicus — Robert Brown of the British Museum*, British Museum, London and Cramer, Braunschweig, 1985.

MAIDEN, J.: *Flora of Norfolk Island*, Sydney, 1904.

MAIDEN, J.: *Sir Joseph Banks, the "Father of Austrralia"*, Government Printer. Sydney, 1909.

MAIDEN, J.: 'Records of Australian Botanists' in *Journal and Proceedings of the Royal Society of New South Wales*, vol.LV. Sydney, 1921.

Bibliography

MEYNELL, G.: 'Francis Bauer, Joseph Banks, Everard Home and others' in *Archives of Natural History*, 11(2), London, 1983, p.209-221.

MOYAL, A.: *'a bright and savage land'* — *Scientists in colonial Australia*, Collins, Sydney, 1986.

NISSEN, C.: *Botanische Prachtwerke — die Blütezeit der Pflanzenillustration von 1740 bis 1840*, Herbert Reichner, Wien, 1933.

SCOTT, E.: *The Life of Captain Matthew Flinders R.N.*, Angus and Robertson, Sydney, 1914.

SMITH, B.: *European Vision and the South Pacific*, Second Edition, Harper and Row, Sydney, (1960).

STAFLEU, F. & COWEN, R.: *Taxonomic literature*, Second Edition, Bohn, Scheltema and Holkema, Utrecht, 1976.

STEARN, W.T.: 'Franz and Ferdinand Bauer, Masters of Botanical Illustration' in *Endeavour*, vol.XIX, no.73, Jan. 1960.

STEARN, W.T. & BLUNT, W. (Eds.): *The Australian Flower Paintings of Ferdinand Bauer*, Basilisk Press, London, 1976.

STEARN, W.T.: *The Natural History Museum at South Kensington*, Heinemann, London, 1981.

WANTRUP, J.: *Australian Rare Books 1788-1900*, Hordern House, Sydney, 1987.

WITTMACK, L.: 'Zwei österreichische Pflanzenmaler in England' in *Beiträge zum landwirtschaftlichen Pflanzenbau*, Parey, Berlin, 1924.

WURZBACH, C.: *Biographisches Lexikon des Kaisertums Österreich*, Zamarski, Vienna, 1856.

Bauer's drawings originally appeared in;

BAUER, F.L.: *Illustrationes Florae Novae Hollandiae, sive icones generum quae in Prodromo Floare Novae Hollandiae et insulae van Diemen descripsit Robertus Brown*, published by the author, London, 1813

ENDLICHER, S.: *Prodromus Florae Norfolkicae*, Vienna, 1833.

ENDLICHER, S.: *Iconographia Generum Plantarum*, Vienna, 1838.

FLINDERS, M.; Atlas of the *Voyage to Terra Australis*, see above.

LAMBERT, A.B.: *A Description of the Genus Pinus*, 2 volumes, London, 1803-24.

LINDLEY, J.: *Digitalium Monographia*, London, 1821.

SIBTHORP, J. & SMITH, J.: *Flora Graeca*, 1806-1840.

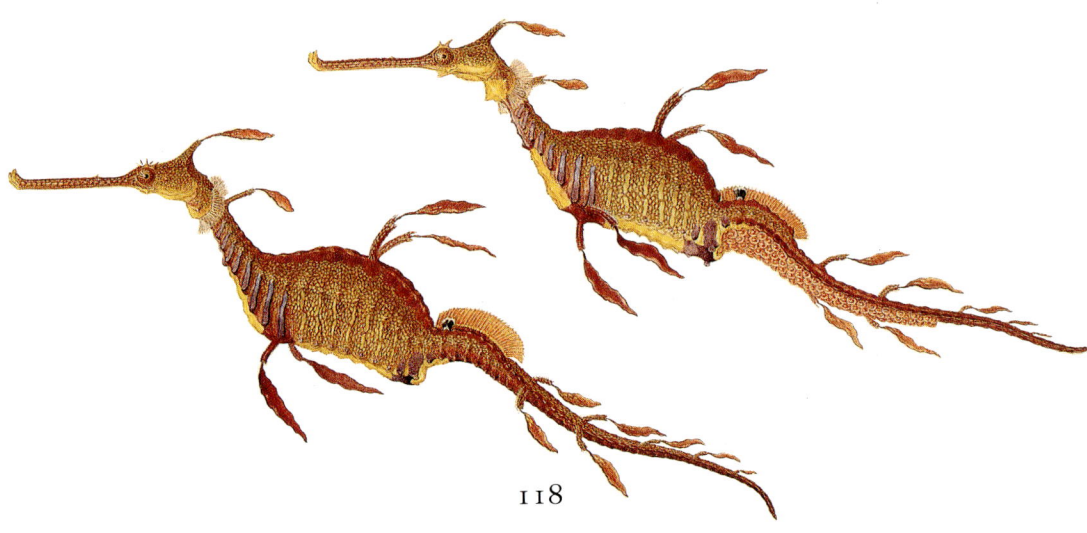

Index

Geographical names, subjects of the drawings and selected institutions have been indexed. Page numbers in **bold** refer to illustrations.

Index